Popular Music

TC

COLIN CRIPPS

edited by
Roy Bennett and Michael Burnett

D0317246

Note to the Teacher

This book is an introduction to the main forms and styles of popular music. It is suitable for year 10 and 11 pupils taking GCSE and could also be used with non-examination pupils of lower age groups.

Each unit of the book deals with a related group of musical styles and discusses their evolution, social background, distinctive musical characteristics and central techniques. Chapter headings are titles of popular songs of the period. The assignments, which illustrate these techniques, require the pupil to respond in a variety of ways. A discography for each style is included at the end of each section, covering background listening. A specially recorded tape, demonstrating the essential techniques of popular music, accompanies the book.

The assignments can be used to build up a folder or tape of music and songs created by the student. Most can be adapted to suit a wide range of both skill and instruments; the only pre-knowledge required of students is a basic musical literacy. (It should be made clear to students that jazz notation is not always exact.)

⟦cassette icon⟧ indicates recorded items

PUBLISHED BY THE PRESS SYNDICATE OF THE UNIVERSITY OF CAMBRIDGE
The Pitt Building, Trumpington Street, Cambridge, United Kingdom

CAMBRIDGE UNIVERSITY PRESS
The Edinburgh Building, Cambridge CB2 2RU, UK
40 West 20th Street, New York, NY 10011–4211, USA
10 Stamford Road, Oakleigh, VIC 3166, Australia
Ruiz de Alarcón 13, 28014 Madrid, Spain
Dock House, The Waterfront, Cape Town 8001, South Africa

http://www.cambridge.org

First published 1988
Fifth printing 2001

Printed in the United Kingdom at the University Press, Cambridge

Book: ISBN 0 521 31884 X
Cassette: ISBN 0 521 26828 1

780.904
R29049

Contents

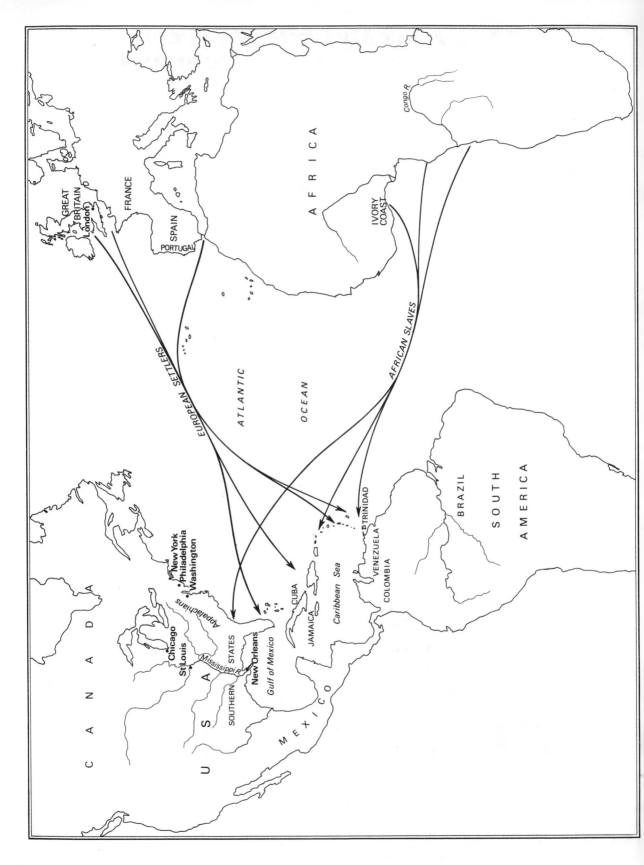

1 Set My Children Free: The music of the slaves

SLAVERY

During the 1600s, while white European settlers were colonizing America, labour was in short supply. White landowners needed large numbers of cheap workers to produce tobacco, rice, sugar and other crops. They got over their problems by buying slaves. These slaves were men, women and children from the West African coastal area, kidnapped from their homes and shipped to America in slave ships. They were chained and crowded together below decks and suffered from disease and lack of water. Of the forty million slaves who were kidnapped in this way, only 15 million arrived in America.

Once in America the slaves were bought and sold, and made to work and live in poor conditions. Punishments were horrifying and the settlers did their best to stop the slaves playing and singing their own African music. The settlers were not successful though; and, in the end, new styles of music were created when the slaves mixed their own African tradition with the European music of the settlers. Examples of these new styles were found in their **work-songs** and **spirituals** (see pages 4 and 5).

AFRICAN AND EUROPEAN MUSIC

There were many differences between the music taken to America by the white Europeans and the music taken there by black African slaves.

Scales

Much European classical music was based on scales made up of seven notes. African scales often used five notes and avoided the small (or semitone) steps which were important in European scales. Assignment 1 will help to make these differences clear. (Classical music scales are called **diatonic** scales. Five-note scales are called **pentatonic** scales.)

'Tight packing' maximized the cargo that a slave ship could carry.

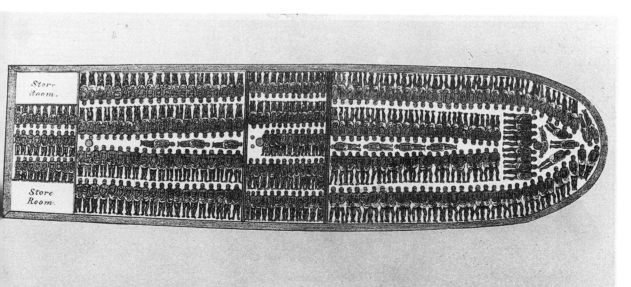

| Assignment 1 | Listen to the differences as you play these scales one after each other. In particular, notice how the five-note scale has no semitones: |

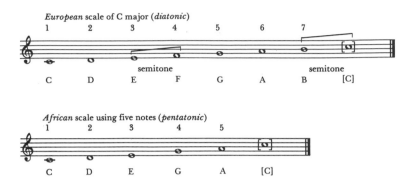

| Assignment 2 | Using any instrument you like, compose a short tune which starts and ends on the note C and uses only the notes of the major diatonic scale. Keep a record of the tune on tape or on manuscript paper. |

| Assignment 3 | Using any instrument you like, compose a short tune which starts and ends on the note C and uses only the notes of the pentatonic scale. Keep a record of the tune on tape or on manuscript paper. |

| Polyrhythm | One of the biggest differences between European and African music is the part played by rhythm. Rhythm is more important in African music, where many different rhythmic ideas are often played simultaneously with exciting effect. Music of this kind is said to be **polyrhythmic**. At local gatherings in Africa one drummer sets up a basic rhythm. Other drummers then join in with different rhythms, which cut across each other to create a complex rhythmic effect. Other instruments and voices, often in several parts, join in too. |

Ewe drummers at a funeral wake, Accra, Ghana.

Assignment 4   Try this experiment.

(a)   Using a metronome or drum-machine to keep the basic time, work
singly, or in small groups, and make up a short rhythmic pattern that
repeats with every four taps of the metronome. Percussion, hand-claps
or tuned instruments playing the note C may be used. Starting with just
the metronome and one group's rhythm, gradually bring in other
groups' rhythms. You are now playing polyrhythmic music.

(b)   Repeat the same experiment but this time sit round in a circle. Each
person invents a rhythm as he or she joins in. By listening to the
rhythms already going on you can build up quite a complicated
polyrhythmic pattern.

*Susu dancer, Sierra Leone,
dancing to the music of a
xylophone band.*

Assignment 5 Repeat these experiments, but this time use only tuned instruments and divide into groups playing the notes C, E, or G.

One last difference between European and African music is in the way each is performed. In African music everyone joins in the performance by playing, singing, clapping, dancing, or simply moving in time to it. European classical music is usually written down by a composer for musicians to perform to an audience which only responds when the music is finished. African music is remembered, not written down, and is often changed during performance.

During slavery, these two kinds of music, African and European, were mixed together in many different ways over a long period of time. One of the first results of this mixture was the **work-song**.

WORK-SONGS Work-songs were invented to help overcome the boredom of hard, monotonous jobs. They had a regular beat which was made to fit the rhythm of the work being done. In quarries, or on road-making gangs, much of the work was done by wielding picks, hammers and shovels to a regular rhythm. The work-song would keep to the beat of the hammers. It would be led by one member of the work gang, with the other members of the gang joining in after him. This is a typically African way of singing songs and is described as

Call-and-response patterning 'call-and-response' patterning. Here is an example of a work-song from after the days of slavery. The leader sings the words and the other members of the gang respond with 'Huh' as they wield their picks or hammers:

Assignment 6 Think of a job done nowadays which could have a work-song made up for it. What do you think the modern singers would be singing about? Why would there be a difference?

Work-songs show some elements of African music clearly. Their melodies cut across the beat, making lively rhythms which sometimes move ahead of it, sometimes behind it. Take a look at the first line of 'Take This Hammer'. The second part of the word 'Hammer' comes before a strong beat:

So does the second part of 'Captain'. This kind of cutting across the beat is called **syncopation** (see page 10).

SPIRITUALS AND GOSPEL Another place where ideas from African and European music were mixed together was in religious music. Plantation owners tried to convert their slaves to Christianity. For many blacks this religion offered hope, as they saw themselves as the children of Israel who would one day be led out of slavery to their promised land. Here are the words of one of the slaves' religious songs. It's called a **spiritual**:

> When Israel was in Egypt's land,
> *Let my people go!*
> Oppressed so hard they could not stand,
> *Let my people go!*
> Go down, Moses, way down in Egypt's land,
> *Tell old Pharoah,*
> *Let my people go!*

Spirituals mixed the syncopations and polyrhythms of Africa with the hymn-tunes the slaves took from the white settlers. The spirituals were based on the African call-and-response patterning, with a leader (in this case, the priest) singing first, then being answered by the rest (the congregation) in chorus. In the example above, the leader would sing the long lines, and the chorus would respond with the short lines, sung in harmony.
Spiritual singing would often turn into a large-scale event with everybody dancing and clapping in time to the music, just as in Africa. (A later term for black spiritual and other religious singing is **gospel** music.)

Assignment 7 Using a metronome or drum-machine to set the beat, invent a short tune for the spiritual 'What Do You Think of Jesus?'. Use only the notes of the pentatonic scale (see pages 1 and 2) and end on C, E, or G. Make up your own rhythms and use call-and-response patterning.

> He had to die for you and me
> *What do you think of Jesus?*
> Hung him up upon a tree
> *What do you think of Jesus?*

HARMONY

Harmony (or a chord) results when two or more notes are played or sung together. The 'response' part of a spiritual is made up of a sequence of sung harmonies. The style of these harmonies was based on the European hymn-tune harmonies which the slaves heard being sung by the white settlers; but the slaves' way of performing the harmonies was livelier and more rhythmic – more African, in fact. On this page is an example of a spiritual. Sing and/or play it, and notice the call-and-response patterning and the kind of harmonies that are used.

Standing in the Need of Prayer,

Negro Spiritual

Work-songs and spirituals – the music of the slaves – resulted from a mixture of African and European musical ideas. Later, this mixture gave rise to jazz and 20th-century popular music.

Music to hear

Afro-American background: *Music of the Diola-Fogny, Senegal*, Folkways FE 432.
Afro-American Drums, Folkways FE 4502.
Work-songs and spirituals: *Murderer's Home*, Pye NJL-11.
Elder Songsters, Music from the South, 6/7, Folkways FP 655/6.

2 Mean, Low Down and Dirty: The beginnings of jazz

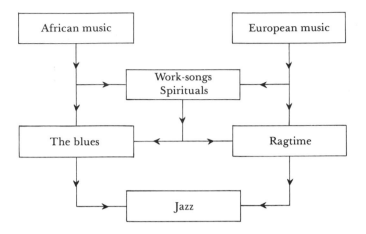

```
┌─────────────────┐                    ┌─────────────────┐
│  African music  │                    │ European music  │
└─────────────────┘                    └─────────────────┘
         │            ┌─────────────┐            │
         │───────────▶│ Work-songs  │◀───────────│
         │            │ Spirituals  │            │
         ▼            └─────────────┘            ▼
┌─────────────────┐          │        ┌─────────────────┐
│   The blues     │◀────────▶│───────▶│    Ragtime      │
└─────────────────┘                   └─────────────────┘
         │            ┌─────────────┐            │
         │───────────▶│    Jazz     │◀───────────│
                      └─────────────┘
```

After slavery was abolished in America in 1865, little changed for most plantation workers. Some freed blacks became valued not just as workers but also as musicians, who would play fiddle or banjo at local dances. Because they were free, these musicians could play their music for anyone who would pay them; so black musicians began playing in theatres and music-halls, and in bars and drinking clubs.

'Plantation' dance in the 1820s before the abolition of slavery.

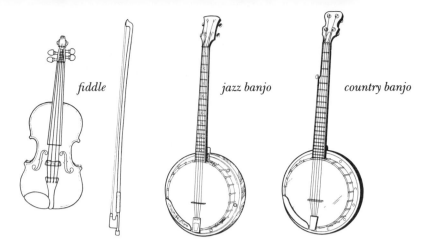

fiddle *jazz banjo* *country banjo*

THE MARCH

One European style of music that had been popular during the 19th century was that of the marching band. The rhythms of a march are neatly divided into a simple count of four beats in a bar. Beats 1 and 3 are accented more strongly than beats 2 and 4.

Assignment 8

While the metronome or drum-machine plays a steady beat, count aloud in sets of 4. On each count of 1 and 3, stamp your feet (or bang a low-sounding drum). On each count of 2 and 4 clap your hands (or hit a snare drum or cymbal). When you have got the march-rhythm going, whistle a well-known march-tune over the top.

It was as a result of the victory by the Northern States in the American civil war that the slaves were freed. With the end of the war many of the marching bands which had led soldiers into battle were broken up and their instruments sold off cheaply. Many blacks took up these instruments – clarinets, trumpets, trombones, side drums, bass drums and cymbals. They formed their own bands and played their own versions of the formal European march-tunes. By introducing syncopated rhythms, and by changing the notes of the tunes when it suited them, they made them more fun to play. In fact they 'jazzed' the tunes up, or 'ragged' them in a new and exciting way.

The effect was thrilling. Over the top of the steady march-rhythm all kinds of crazy things were now happening. The notes were being 'bent' (deliberately played slightly below pitch). The notes started and ended in unusual places, and sometimes entirely different notes were being substituted. The musicians were inventing their parts as they went along.

trombone *clarinet* *trumpet*

9

RAGTIME

The first style of popular music to include some of these exciting new techniques was **ragtime**. Ragtime was played on the piano. It developed during the 1890s in the saloons, gambling halls, cafés and brothels of the cities in the Southern States of the USA. Ragtime was the first black music to be accepted by the white people, and white people finally came to play and write it themselves. It is similar to classical music in the sense that it is composed and written down, not developed during performance or simply remembered from hearing others play it.

It is similar to march music as well, with the beats being quavers. The pianist's left hand picks out the bass drum and cymbal rhythm. Look at this piece of music.

'Frog Legs Rag'

James Scott

You will see that the part written in the bass clef, played by the left hand, has a regular rhythm pattern. First it plays two notes an octave apart and then it usually plays either a chord of three notes or another octave pair. Rhythmically, the octave notes take the place of the bass drum and the chords take the place of the cymbal. Notice that the chord is higher in pitch than the lowest of the octave notes. This gives a rhythmic effect which makes ragtime easily recognisable.

Syncopation

The influence of **syncopation** in ragtime is clearly heard in the part played by the pianist's right hand. Notice how in 'Frog Legs Rag' some notes are sounded just before the beat (look for the notes that are tied together in the music). At other times there are rests on strong beats. This effect, as we've seen, is called 'syncopation'. It remains one of the basic effects of popular music even today.

The structure of ragtime

Ragtime has a regular overall shape: a piece of ragtime has four or more melodies or themes, each lasting for 16 bars, which we can call A, B, C and D. The melodies are often played in this order:

A A B B A C C D D.

Scott Joplin (1868–1917), the key figure in the development of ragtime in the early 1900s. His Maple Leaf Rag *quickly sold a million copies.*

By syncopating familiar dances such as the jig, the reel and the hoedown the music became 'ragged'. The dance step that resulted became the 'rag'.

Scott Joplin is the best-known ragtime composer. Born in 1868 near Marshall, Texas, he played the piano for years in brothels and saloons. He finally had success with tunes like 'Maple Leaf Rag' and 'The Entertainer'.

Assignment 9

Listen to 'Maple Leaf Rag' by Scott Joplin - on *Piano Rags* volume 1 (H71248). See how many different themes you can pick out. Write down the order in which they are played.

Some poor-quality music that wasn't really ragtime came to be called by that name because ragtime had become a money-spinning business. This was particularly true of the sales of the card 'rolls' which controlled the new mechanical pianos, called pianolas. These instruments were the equivalent of today's juke-boxes, playing popular tunes after coins were inserted.

THE BLUES

Another style of early black music was **the blues**. This was a folk music that grew out of the same mixture of African and European ideas which produced work-songs and spirituals. Like these, the blues told of the feelings, fears and hopes of the singers – but it did so in a more personal way. It began, as did much black music, in the country districts of the South; but before long blues singers could be found in the cities, too.

Originally the blues was performed by one singer usually accompanied by a guitar, or banjo, and occasionally by a piano. Its rhythms were more varied than those of ragtime. It was a raw-sounding music, full of emotion; and the scale upon which its melodies and harmonies were based came to be called the **blues scale**.

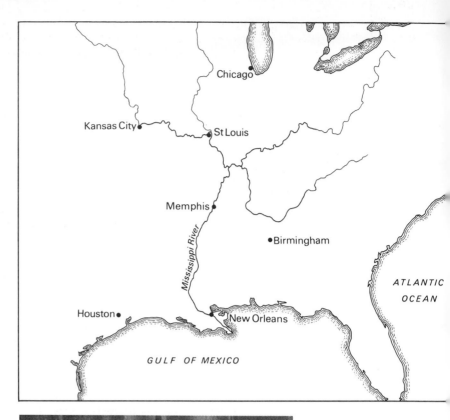

USA, the South: home of the blues.

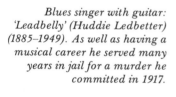

Blues singer with guitar: 'Leadbelly' (Huddie Ledbetter) (1885–1949). As well as having a musical career he served many years in jail for a murder he committed in 1917.

The blues scale	This is a version of the major diatonic scale (see page 2) in which the third and seventh steps are played or sung below pitch. This produces a deliberately out of tune ('bent') effect which helps give the blues its special flavour.

'blue' note   'blue' note

Slide guitar	The sliding of notes out of tune was often heightened by the singer half-speaking and half-singing. This was imitated by guitarists playing the guitar with a bottle-neck or 'slide'. The 'slide' is a tube which is fitted over one of the guitarist's fingers on the left hand and is then slid up and down the strings while they are plucked with the right hand. The guitar has to be especially tuned for this.
Assignment 10	Tune the strings of a guitar either (1) to D, A, D, F♯, A, D, or (2) to E, B, E, G♯, B, E (lowest to highest). Use a piece of copper tubing and slide it over the strings of the guitar. See what effects you can create by sliding it between the open strings and the third, fifth, seventh, tenth, and twelfth frets. Contrast single notes with whole chords (strumming across some or all the strings together).
THE 12-BAR BLUES	Innumerable blues songs are built up in the **12-bar blues** form. The form has also been used by popular musicians throughout the 20th century. Most blues verses have three lines, the first two being the same:

> It was early this morning that I had my trial.
> It was early this morning that I had my trial.
> Ninety days on the county road, and the judge didn't even smile.

In the 12-bar blues each of these lines takes four bars:

Line 1 $\frac{4}{4}$ / / / / | / / / / | / / / / | / / / / |

Line 2 / / / / | / / / / | / / / / | / / / / |

Line 3 / / / / | / / / / | / / / / | / / / / |

Assignment 11	Listen to one of the blues albums listed at the end of the chapter and see how many 12-bar versions you discover. It will help if you count out the bar numbers in each case.
Chords	The 12-bar blues makes use of three chords. The technical names for these chords are the *tonic* (or chord I), the *subdominant* (or chord IV) and the *dominant* (or chord V). Look once again at the scale of C major:

Note:	C	D	E	F	G	A	B	C
Chord:	I	II	III	IV	V	VI	VII	I
Name:	tonic	supertonic	mediant	subdominant	dominant	submediant	leading note	tonic

Each note of the scale has its own basic chord. This consists of the main note, together with the notes which form a 3rd and a 5th above it. The main note – the note of the scale on which the chord is built – is called the *root* of the chord. It is from this note that the chord takes its name. Here are the three main chords used in the 12-bar blues:

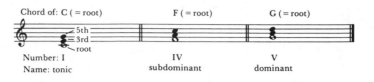

Chord of: C (= root)	F (= root)	G (= root)
Number: I	IV	V
Name: tonic	subdominant	dominant

Assignment 12

Play these chords on whatever instrument or group of instruments is available. These three chords form the basis not only of the 12-bar blues but of much other popular music as well.

The 12-bar chord structure

In a 12-bar blues the chords are played in a set order. Here is one such order:

bar:	①	②	③	④
lyrics:	I had a dream	that I was	dead. _____	
chords: 4/4	/ / / /	/ / / /	/ / / /	/ / / /
	C(I)	C	C	C

⑤	⑥	⑦	⑧
I had a dream	that I was	dead. _____	
/ / / /	/ / / /	/ / / /	/ / / /
F(IV)	F	C	C

⑨	⑩	⑪	⑫
Evil spirits	all around my	bed. _____	
/ / / /	/ / / /	/ / / /	/ / / /
G(V)	F	C	C

Assignment 13

Divide into small groups with a mixture of instruments. Play the accompaniment to the blues above. Play a straight four beats of the chord for each bar. Those playing melody instruments which can only play one note at a time, not whole chords, should each pick a different note to play for each chord. For example, for the chord of C (I) one player should play the note C, another the note E, and a third the note G. When the chord changes to the chord of F (IV), players change to the notes F, A and C respectively; when the chord of G (V) is to be played they use the notes G, B, and D. Practise the sequence of notes until you can play the accompaniment without looking at the book. (For guitarists *only*, the blues chord sequence is most easily played in the key of E major. The chords then become E (I), A (IV) and B (V).)

Assignment 14

When you are completely familiar with the blues accompaniment compose your own blues melody in the key of C major. Use E♭ (E flat) and B♭ (B flat) to suggest the blues scale and end on the note C. Remember also that the first two lines of music are the same, so you have only two separate lines of melody to write.

*The interior of a slave shanty
in the 1850s.*

Assignment 15   Record a blues accompaniment in C major. Then play or sing your blues melody over your recorded accompaniment. (Save your recording for use in assignment 22.)

Blues lyrics   Here are some examples of blues lyrics:

1. *You can't sleep in my bed*
    You'd better be gone when my man comes in.
    You'd better be gone when my man comes in.
    Stop shaking your tail, 'cos I don't know where
    you've been.

2. *Poor man's blues*
    While you're living in your mansion, you don't know
    what hard times mean.
    While you're living in your mansion, you don't know
    what hard times mean.
    Poor working man's wife is starving; your wife is
    living like a queen.

The words of these blues are simple, honest and strongly felt. They are about the singer's life. Some of the words have double meanings of a sexual nature. Some are about being poor, some about religion and sin, and others about places the singer has been to or wants to go to.

Assignment 16   Put lyrics to your blues song. Write several verses on a subject you feel strongly about. If you are writing about something which doesn't actually involve you, imagine that it does; write your song as if you are a central character in what is going on.

15

Canal Street, New Orleans, in the early 1900s. In the foreground a cart laden with cotton bales.

Blues singers

There are many well-known blues singers from country blues days. These include Huddie Ledbetter (Leadbelly), Blind Blake, Blind Lemon Jefferson, Skip James, Jesse Fuller and many more. Perhaps the best-loved by modern musicians is Robert Johnson. Johnson only recorded around 30 songs, accompanying himself on slide guitar, but many are classic blues like 'Hellhound on my trail' and 'Come on in my kitchen'. Johnson died in 1938 at the age of 26. He had been poisoned.

TRADITIONAL JAZZ (DIXIELAND JAZZ)

The last style of black music to emerge from the African–European musical mixture after 1900 was traditional or 'trad' jazz. Jazz is generally thought to have reached its complete shape in New Orleans (see map on page 12). New Orleans was a large sea-port and the home of many ex-slaves who brought with them work-songs and exciting spiritual music. White people's music was also popular in the form of marches, hymns and sets of dances like the quadrille. Ragtime and blues in their early form could also be heard in New Orleans and instruments were around in plenty. New Orleans was a wild place, like most large ports, and it had a red-light district called Storyville which was full of bars and brothels. The bands that performed in these bars usually had six members. Between them they played cornet, clarinet, trombone, banjo or piano, string bass and drums – instruments typical of a marching band, plus a piano.

16

hi-hat

snare drum

bass drum

side drum
(also called the *floor tom-tom*)

The drum kit In a marching band each drum is carried and played by a different musician. As musicians were paid for playing in bars, employing more than one drummer would have been far too costly; and so one musician had to play all the drums and other percussion instruments. To make his job easier the modern drum kit was developed.

The bass drum and the clashing cymbals (hi-hat) are played with foot pedals and the rest of the kit is played with sticks. This calls for some intricate acts of co-ordination on the part of the drummer.

Assignment 17 Do the following exercise on a drum kit, if you have one, or on different sounding surfaces - table tops, large tins, and so on - if you haven't. Stamp and clap in time with a regular count as shown:

Right foot - count ☐1 2 ☐3 4   Right hand - ☐1 ☐& ☐2 ☐& ☐3 ☐& ☐4 ☐&

Left foot - count   ☐1 ☐2 ☐3 ☐4   Left hand - 1   ☐2   3   ☐4

Tricky, isn't it?

IMPROVISATION What was exciting about the music of these saloon bar bands was the fact that much of it was improvised - made up by the musicians as they went along. This does not mean that tunes had no shape, that everybody just played any notes they felt like, because the result would have been an awful noise. Each piece of music was based on a song which had a march-rhythm as its foundation. The tempo varied greatly from song to song. The chords which formed the accompaniment to the song - often a 12-bar blues or some other sequence from a well-known tune of the time - were already familiar, as were the scales that could be used. The musicians 'played around' with notes of the tunes, and also added counter-melodies, so that they moved further and further away from the original, while still keeping something recognisable. 'Playing around' with, or 'improvising' on tunes such as 'Oh When the Saints Go Marching In' can be done in several ways:

1. The notes of the melody can stay the same but their *length* can be altered.

17

Assignment 18   Here are the first two lines of 'Oh When the Saints Go Marching In'.

Count 1 2 3 & 4 & 1 2 3 & 4 & 1 2 3 & 4 & 1 2 3 4 1 2 3 4

C E F G   C E F G   C E F G E C E   D

(a)   Learn to play it as written. Use a metronome or drum-machine to give the beat as you play.

(b)   Playing the same notes in the same order, change the tune by altering the length of some of the notes.

(c)   Repeat (a) and (b) above with any song of your choice. A nursery rhyme is often a good place to start.

2.   Extra notes can be added to the tune.

Assignment 19

Play the first line of 'Oh When the Saints' but this time make the first two G notes (♩) much shorter and add an extra piece of tune of your own between the G and the C. Use any of the notes C, E, F, G, A, to make up this tune. You do not have to use each note and you can use any of them more than once.

The Eagle Jazz Band, New Orleans, 1916.

Assignment 20

3. Notes can be taken out of the tune.
See how many notes can be taken away from 'Oh When the Saints' before making the tune unrecognisable.

4. A fourth way of improvising on a tune is to use the same pattern of note values – the exact rhythm of the original tune – but now with the notes arranged in a different order.

Assignment 21

Tap out the rhythm of 'Oh When the Saints' on a table top. Use the notes from the tune (C E F G) and fit them to the tapped rhythm of the melody – but in a different order. The result should be recognisable from the length of each note, but the tune will be different.

There are many more difficult and subtle ways of improvising on a tune. A jazz musician doesn't think about these, but plays from 'feel' or natural instinct. It is often more difficult for a jazz musician to play a tune 'straight', or exactly as it's written down, because it feels stiff and unnatural.

Assignment 22
Improvise a blues melody in C major against the backing you made in assignment 15. Use the blues scale with its E♭ and B♭.

Imagine the effect on an audience of a jazz band improvising on well-known folk songs, marches and dance tunes. In a 'trad' jazz band, it was not just one
member of the band who improvised – everybody did it. The result was fun and exciting.

It was a white band – the Original Dixieland Jazz Band – that made the first jazz recording in 1916. The technique of recording music was new at this time and the quality of recordings was poor; but there was money to be made from the sale of records and techniques were improved. To begin with, it was mainly white musicians who were able to get their music recorded.

Migration north

By the end of World War I (1914–18) the influence of jazz had spread across America. The river boats which travelled up and down the Mississippi from New Orleans took jazz upstream to Chicago, where it found another home, along with the blues. As the black population moved north looking for work, black music moved with them.

Louis Armstrong took his New Orleans jazz to Chicago in 1922. He was a brilliant trumpet player and his improvisations soon dominated the music of the bands he played in. Blues and jazz were to develop with the move north; but by now ragtime had come to a musical dead-end.

Music to hear

Ragtime: *Piano Rags by Scott Joplin*, Vols. 1–3, Nonesuch H71248, H71264, H71305.

Blues: *King of the Delta Blues Singers*, Robert Johnson, CBS UK62456.

The Story of the Blues, CBS 66218.

Screening the Blues, CBS 63288.

The Country Blues, Vols. 1 and 2, RBF Records RF 1/9.

Traditional jazz: *Kid Ory*, Vol. 2, Good Time Jazz EPG11171.

King Oliver's Creole Jazz Band 1923, Riverside RLP8805.

King of New Orleans Jazz, Vols. 1 and 2, RCA RD 27113; RCA RD 27184.

Cylinder Jazz: 1897–1928, Saydisc SDL112.

Hot Jazz, Pop Jazz, Hokum and Hilarity, RCA RD 7807.

3 Take the 'A' Train: Jazz travels north

The migration of black people northwards, in particular to the cities, continued throughout the 1920s and 1930s, speeded up by the great depression (1929). Floods and pestilence had hit the crops in the South, while the Northern cities and their industries offered so many opportunities. In the 1890s, 80% of black Americans lived in the rural South. By 1920 the figure was 65% and by 1950 only 20% were living there. Immigration of white Europeans almost stopped during World War I and blacks were in demand to fill the jobs.

Sadly, blacks were restricted to living in certain areas of the cities and as more poured in these areas stayed the same size. Soon each city had its own overcrowded black ghettos made up of families sharing apartments and facilities. The jobs the blacks got were poorly paid and unpleasant. During the depression, jobs were scarce and black people continued to live in poverty. Yet it was in such circumstances that new black music styles were to develop.

During the 1920s the black band-leader Fletcher Henderson began the trend towards bigger jazz bands. With 10 or more players, instead of the previous five or so, these bands needed more organising. So a member of the band acted as *arranger*, writing down much of the music so that it could be played without the kind of clashes that would happen if all the musicians improvised at once.

tenor saxophone

Many white band-leaders followed Fletcher Henderson's example, and dance-halls became larger to cope with the new big bands. The 'composed' jazz they played was well suited to dancing, and the sound the bands made was less energetic than that of earlier bands. The new jazz sound became known as **swing**.

SWING

A 'swing band' consisted of 15 or more players. It included saxophones, and by now the banjo had been superseded by the guitar. This was the common line-up:

Brass: 3 trumpets, 3 trombones
Reeds: clarinet, 2 alto saxophones, 2 tenor saxophones
Rhythm: piano, guitar, string bass, drums.

Riffs and chords

Instruments from the brass and reed sections took turns at solo improvising while the other instruments harmonised with each other, or played a *riff* in the background.

A riff is a melodic and/or harmonic phrase, which is repeated persistently throughout part or all of a piece of music. The chords played by the band were now becoming more complicated. These chords included more notes and had a generally more 'mellow' (rich and smooth) sound

21

*Big band in the 1920s. The dancer
in the centre is Edward Kennedy
'Duke' Ellington. He later formed
his own band and became internationally famous as a composer,
arranger and band-leader.*

<table>
<tr><td>**Chromatic
scales**</td><td>The scales used in swing were more complicated than those used before in jazz. Often, not only was the blues scale used, but also 'chromatic' scales.</td></tr>
</table>

A chromatic scale is one which proceeds entirely by semitones. For example: beginning on C, instead of just using the piano white keys (C, D, E, F, G, A, B, C,) or a mixture of certain white and black keys like the blues scale (C, D, Eb, F, G, A, Bb, C), the chromatic scale includes *all* the white and black keys:

Notes of the
chromatic scale:

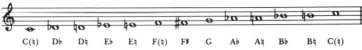

C(♮) Db D♮ Eb E♮ F(♮) F♯ G Ab A♮ Bb B♮ C(♮)

Freely using any or all of these notes makes both melodies and improvisations more complex. Here is an example of a melody using 10 of the 12 notes of the chromatic scale. The key signature tells us that the notes B and E are flattened unless shown otherwise:

Caravan   Duke Ellington

Assignment 23

Look at the melody of 'Caravan' by Duke Ellington above. Make a list of all the different notes you can find. Which notes from the chromatic scale are missing?

The actual shapes, or forms, of tunes from the swing era are probably the most straightforward things about them. They were often based on the 12-bar blues form or on the popular song form.

**POPULAR SONG
FORM**

Popular song form is commonly 32 bars long. These 32 bars are divided into 4 sections of 8 bars each. The first 2 sections, and the last section, use the same melody which we will call melody A. The third section has a different melody which we'll call melody B. Each section coincides with a line of words. So the form or shape of the music can be expressed as A A B A.

Turn to the next page for a good example of this structure – George Gershwin's 'I Got Rhythm'.

Lyrics

Line 1

I got	rhythm.	I got	music.	I got	my man. Who could	ask for anything	more?
Melody A / / / /	/ / / /	/ / / /	/ / / /	/ / / /	/ / / /	/ / / /	/ / / /
Bars: 1	2	3	4	5	6	7	8

Line 2

I got	daisies	in green	pastures.	I got	my man. Who could	ask for anything	more?
Melody A / / / /	/ / / /	/ / / /	/ / / /	/ / / /	/ / / /	/ / / /	/ / / /
Bars: 9	10	11	12	13	14	15	16

Line 3

Old Man	Trouble	I don't	mind him.	You won't	find him	round my	door.
Melody B / / / /	/ / / /	/ / / /	/ / / /	/ / / /	/ / / /	/ / / /	/ / / /
Bars: 17	18	19	20	21	22	23	24

Line 4

I got	starlight.	I got	sweet dreams.	I got	my man. Who could	ask for anything	more?
Melody A / / / /	/ / / /	/ / / /	/ / / /	/ / / /	/ / / /	/ / / /	/ / / /
Bars: 25	26	27	28	29	30	31	32

Assignment 24

Listen to 'I Got Rhythm' (on *Ella Fitzgerald sings The George and Ira Gershwin Songbook*, Verve Records POL 395-2615063). Count the number of bars for each line of the verse. Remember there are four beats to each bar. Work out how the A A B A structure fits.

Assignment 25

(a) Listen to the following melody and follow it on the written score. Write down the bar number where each A and B section begins.

Take the 'A' Train

Billy Strayhorn

(b) The melody is based on the chromatic scale. Which notes of the chromatic scale (as it is written on page 23) are used?

Assignment 26

Compose your own song in A A B A form. First compose a melody 8 bars long using the C major scale again if you like (see page 2). Next, compose another melody line of the same length. Start this second melody line on note 4 of the scale. (In C major this will be F.) Now sing and/or play the first line twice, followed by the second line once, and then return to the first line.

Swing rhythms

The rhythm of swing was also more complicated than that of trad jazz. Latin American and Caribbean rhythms began to be used. These rhythms developed from the mixture of African polyrhythms and the music of the whites who settled in these areas.

Here are some of the rhythms that became popular in the dance music of the 1920s, 1930s and 1940s, and which were used by the jazz musicians:

Samba (Brazilian)

Rumba (Afro-Spanish)

Charleston (Afro-American)

Beguine (Caribbean)

(> = stressed or accented note)

Assignment 27

Tap out the above rhythms. It will help to listen to records like 'Begin the Beguine' by Cole Porter performed by the Andrews Sisters (Capitol LCT 6132) or *Ron Goodwin Conducts the New Zealand Symphony Orchestra* (EMI/Columbia EJ26 01721) or 'The Charleston' by James P. Johnson and Cecil Mack, *The Charleston Days* (Flapper PAST 706) and *The Dance Band Years (the 1920s)* (Saville SVL169). These rhythms can often be found on electronic keyboard instruments and rhythm units.

BE-BOP

In the swing heyday of the 1930s many bands attracted large audiences of fans when they played in dance halls and cinemas; in fact, sometimes it was difficult to hear the instruments over the screams of the fans. But by the end of World War II (in 1945) swing had had its day. Young black musicians, feeling that jazz had lost its spontaneity, created a new style called **be-bop** which became popular during the 1940s and 1950s.

Be-bop was played by small bands and was based on fast, complicated improvisation. It also used complicated chords and rhythms. But in the end so few people could play or appreciate be-bop that it ceased to be truly popular music. Be-bop musicians included Dizzy Gillespie and Miles Davis.

COOL JAZZ

During the 1950s, white musicians like Dave Brubeck brought influences from classical music into jazz. They also used more harmonies that were new to jazz and often preferred 5 or 11 beats to a bar rather than the standard four.

Assignment 28

Listen to Dave Brubeck's hit 'Take Five' (This can be found on *Brubeck's Greatest Hits*, CBS 32046). Clap out the $\frac{5}{4}$ rhythm which the music uses:

Count 1 2 3 4 5 | 1 2 3 4 5 | 1 2 3 4 5   etc.

This style became known as 'cool' jazz because it was generally more mellow sounding, and less 'dynamic' than be-bop; it too was usually played by small groups of musicians. Cool jazz also failed to get much popular attention.

CITY BLUES

The blues also found its way north and west to the big cities where it became known as **city blues**. During the depression (1930s), record sales had slumped and one of the main forms of entertainment for blacks was the 'house rent party' where dances were held in people's houses. At this time the dance music was usually provided by a pianist as bands were too big and too expensive.

Jazz pianist and composer Jelly Roll Morton who learned his skills playing in the brothels of Storyville, New Orleans.

BOOGIE-WOOGIE

The pianists played a style of piano blues based on the 12-bar chord pattern (see page 14). This was called 'boogie-woogie' and used wild and syncopated rhythms. These exciting rhythms were played over a basic rhythm which is usually written like this:

Count 1(a&)a 2(a&)a 3(a&)a 4(a&)a

In fact the true rhythm is closer to this:

Assignment 29

Tap out the boogie-woogie rhythm shown above.

This basic boogie-woogie rhythm was played by the pianist's left hand while he improvised wildly using the blues scale with the right hand. The left-hand part usually changed very little. It either featured a pattern of single notes or a driving chord-rhythm.

Assignment 30

(a) Here is a single note boogie bass pattern in the key of C major. Learn to play it. Write out the same pattern, but starting on F instead of C; then again, starting on G.

(b) Use this bass pattern as an accompaniment for a 12 bar blues. As each phrase takes two bars you must change your starting note at the right time. For a 12-bar blues in C major you begin your bass pattern on C for a C chord, on F for an F chord and on G for a G chord:

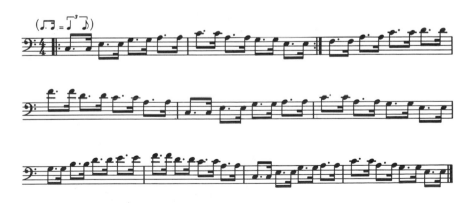

(c) Keeping the same rhythm, and the same key (C major), find a different series of notes to make your walking bass. You can make your pattern just one bar in length if you wish.

electric guitar

Muddy Waters Blues Band in performance in 1968. Born in 1915, Waters received late but well-deserved international recognition when the Rolling Stones recorded versions of his songs.

Assignment 31   Here is a driving boogie-woogie chord-rhythm. This time the key is G major:

Copy out the chord-rhythm shown above. Write out the same pattern in the key of C major. Learn to play it.

In time, the blues pianist was joined by musicians playing double bass, drums, guitar and harmonica. By the 1940s amplifiers had become available and the guitar, harmonica and vocals could be boosted in volume. City blues was now loud, fast – and popular.

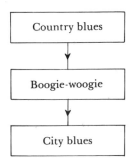

```
┌──────────────────┐
│   Country blues  │
└──────────────────┘
          │
          ▼
┌──────────────────┐
│   Boogie-woogie  │
└──────────────────┘
          │
          ▼
┌──────────────────┐
│    City blues    │
└──────────────────┘
```

xas guitarist T-Bone Walker was
e of the first city blues players to
e an amplified guitar on record.
is picture was taken in London,
in 1968.

Texas guitarist T-Bone Walker was one of the first city blues players to use an amplified guitar on record. This picture was taken in London, in 1968.

It was a city blues musician, T-Bone Walker, who pioneered the rock-guitar sound and technique. Walker used to turn his electric-guitar amplifier up to distortion level. This creates what is known as a *dirty* sound. At this volume, single notes could be played on the electric guitar and bc as loud as any other instrument; notes could also be held for as long as the guitarist wanted, just by trembling a finger across the frets. This is called *finger tremolo* or *vibrato*. The city blues style produced many famous guitar soloists like B.B. King, Freddie King and Buddy Guy.

Other city blues stars included harmonica players Junior Wells and Little Walter, the pianist Otis Spann and singers Sonny Boy Williamson, Howling Wolf and Muddy Waters – plus Willie Dixon, the songwriter and bass player.

During the 1940s and 1950s city blues was the most popular music in the clubs, bars, dance-halls and street-corner cafés in the black areas of American cities. There were special record labels for city blues music, although the music was never distributed through the major, white-owned, record companies.

Music to hear

Swing:
The Age of Ellington, RCA PL 42086.
Golden Hour of Glenn Miller, Golden Hour GH831.
Jumping at the Woodside, Count Basie, Golden Hour GH873.
Jazz Anthology – From King Oliver to Ornette Coleman, CBS (includes examples of popular song form).

Boogie-woogie:
Honky Tonk Train, Meade Lux Lewis, Riverside RLP8806.
Barrelhouse Blues and Boogie Woogie, 1 & 2, Storyville SLP 1551.

City blues:
The Great Blues Men, Golden Hour GH864.
Buddy Guy and Junior Wells play the blues, Atlantic K40240.
Chess Blues Masters, Muddy Waters, Chess NL6641 639 2ACBM 203.
T-Bone Blues, Atlantic UK K40131.
B.B. King Story, Blue Horizon 7 63216.
South Side Blues Piano, London AL3536.

4 Nashville Skyline: From folk to country and western

Another branch of American popular music developed during the 20th Century, from the music of the poor white people. It began as folk music and finally became country music or **country and western**.

FOLK MUSIC

Folk music arrived in North America with the earliest white settlers and was mainly based on English, Scottish and Irish traditional music. As time passed, the folk music of America and that of the British Isles developed in different ways, yet kept much in common.

Folk music was the music with which people entertained themselves and each other. It was seldom written down and both tunes and words were passed down through the generations, changing slightly all the time.

BALLADS

'White' folk songs were based on melodies and storylines. The dramatic stories they told were often long, and were about lovers, deceived husbands, sailors and soldiers gone away to war, the cycle of the seasons, magical characters and events. These songs were called **ballads**.

DANCE MUSIC

The dance-tunes brought by the settlers were more rhythmic than ballads. In the British Isles dance music was performed mainly on the fiddle and accordion, or on a wind instrument like the bagpipes, the whistle or the flute. By 1900, in America, the fiddle and the banjo were the most popular dance-music instruments. There were several different types of folk-dance. One of these was the jig, which is in ⁶⁄₈ time with the following rhythm:

Jig   ⁶⁄₈ ♩ ♪♩ ♪

Count 1 2 3 2 2 3

Poor whites dancing to the music of banjos and fiddles in rural Virginia in the 1920s.

Other folk-dance rhythms were: the reel, the strathspey and the rant, which are all in $\frac{4}{4}$ time; the hornpipe and the polka, which are in $\frac{2}{4}$ time; the waltz, in $\frac{3}{4}$ time; and the slip jig in $\frac{9}{8}$ time.

Modes

The melodies of folk ballads and dances were based on a set of scales called **modes**, which had been in use for centuries. Here are some of them, written out using the white notes of the piano keyboard. Notice that it's the position of the semitones in each mode which gives it its character.

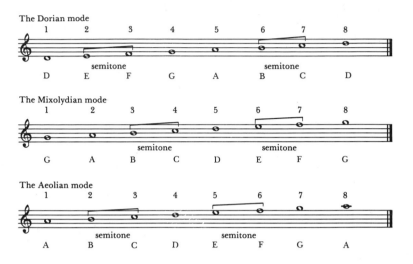

Assignment 32

Copy out the melody of any well-known tune you can find which is in the key of C major. Learn to play it. Then change the notes so that the tune is in the Dorian mode: that is, so that any note C in the original version becomes note D in the new version, note D in the original becomes note E and so on. Now play the new, Dorian, version of the tune. How has it changed? Is it still recognisable?

Assignment 33

Compose a four-line tune using either the Aeolian mode or the Mixolydian mode. Try to compose the tune so that it fits to the words of this verse of an old folk ballad:

> A sailor's life is a merry life.
> They rob young girls of their heart's delight,
> Leaving them behind to sigh and mourn,
> They never know when they will return.

In parts of America, such as the Appalachian mountains, this kind of folk music lives on; but in the Southern States a new style has developed from folk-dance rhythms. This new style is called **bluegrass**.

BLUEGRASS

Bluegrass or **hillbilly** is the folk music of poor white people in Virginia, North and South Carolina, Kentucky and Arkansas. The name was first given to the music during the 1950s. Electric instruments are not used in bluegrass. Its main instrument is the banjo which plays the lead usually with

a guitarist strumming chords as a background. Fiddles, mandolin and string bass are also commonly used.

Bluegrass songs are written in the old folk modes with the traditional four-line verse. They are usually about unsuccessful love but themes also include home life, disasters and religion.

This music was played on river boats, at farming tent shows, at home social dances and at conventions. By 1953 it had reached the peak of its popularity as radio gave the music exposure across the USA. As a result, banjo player Earl Scruggs became internationally known.

Ballad singers

Another style of folk music that became popular during the 1940s and 1950s was the modern version of the old folk ballad (see page 31) and its main artist was Woody Guthrie. Ballad singers usually accompanied themselves on the guitar or banjo, and sang new versions of the four-line-verse traditional song. While the melodies were simple, and used European major or modal scales, the lyrics told stories about people and their social problems or disasters that affected them. When, as a result of bad farming methods, strong winds blew away most of the topsoil in the state of Tennessee leaving thousands of families ruined, Guthrie wrote and recorded a collection of songs called the Dust-Bowl Ballads telling the world of their plight and urging the government to help. Guthrie was the first 'protest singer' to become popular; he was followed by Pete Seeger, Joan Baez, Bob Dylan and many others.

33

Woody Guthrie, born in Oklahoma in 1912, became the voice of the poor and dispossessed in America. Putting new words to traditional melodies from Oklahoma and Texas he expressed his anger at the political system which had caused such misery.

Assignment 34

Write a set of lyrics which tell the story of some present-day disaster. Each verse should have four lines.

WESTERN SWING

Western swing, which became popular as a dance music in the South-western States during the 1930s and 1940s, was a strange mixture of folk-ballad-style tunes and Dixieland or trad jazz. The 'inventor' of this black/white mix was Bob Willis, the leader of a south-western string band in the 1930s. Western bands featured fiddle, guitar, bass, drums, saxophone, trumpet and vocals, and, like hillbilly, remained popular until the mid-1950s.

COUNTRY AND WESTERN

Country music is the main form of popular music to this day in the Southern States. It has developed throughout the century taking elements of all the other forms of folk music mentioned above. From the folk ballad it has taken the idea that a song should tell a story. It has taken some of its themes from bluegrass and added some of its own. These now include railroads, truckers, good boys or girls gone wrong, romance, heartbreak, disasters and religion. The themes usually have a simple moral message, treated sentimentally, and a cowboy or outlaw feel, which was picked up from the 'cowboy' songs of Gene Autry, Roy Rogers, Tex Ritter and other Hollywood 'singing cowboys' of the 1930s and 1940s. As well as the singing cowboys, the simple tunes are derived from folk songs and from western swing band tunes. Some country songs have the feeling of gospel songs sung and played in a light and relaxed manner.

Nowadays country music has borrowed the electric instruments of rock but, in its first period of staggering national popularity, which peaked in the 1950s, the line-up would include some or all of the following acoustic instruments: guitar, bass, drums, fiddle, banjo, mandolin and pedal steel guitar. It is the pedal steel guitar which gives the 'Hawaiian' sound to many country records. The combined sound of the instruments of a country and western band is clear-cut and lacks distortion.

Gene Autry was one of the 'singing cowboys' who became enormously popular in the 1930s and 1940s.

pedal steel guitar

Although the singing is sometimes syncopated, and the songs are sometimes structured rather like a 12-bar blues, there are few African elements in country music. It is white music, played in the bars, truckers cafés, juke-box joints and country dance-halls of much of rural and working-class America.

Country rhythms

Basically, there are three types of country rhythm now. The first is the fast *shuffle beat*, used for numbers influenced by hillbilly music. Here the basic accompaniment on drums and rhythm guitar revolves around an *alternating-bass* pattern, the whole accompaniment sounding like a large-scale version of the part played by the left hand of a ragtime piano player.

Here is an example using chords I, IV and V in the key of C major (see page 14). These three chords are the basic chords of country music.

Notice that the bass note is followed by a chord and that the bass note changes each time between the root note of the chord and another note from the chord. This is where the name 'alternating bass' comes from. There are many variations which can be made on this basic idea by putting in short runs of notes and walking-bass patterns.

Assignment 35

Work out an alternating-bass pattern for chords I, IV and V in the keys of D major, G major and A major. (Start by writing out the scale for each of these keys, putting in sharps, where needed, to produce the semitone between steps 3 and 4, and 7 and 8 – see page 2.)

The second main type of country rhythm is a slower version of this beat which goes along with the more relaxed main-stream country song.

The third main type is the country waltz. It is in $\frac{3}{4}$ time and has a version of the alternating-bass guitar accompaniment:

Assignment 36

Write out the chords and bass notes shown above in the keys of D major, E major and A major. Notice that the bass note changes at the beginning of each bar, so you need two bars of each chord to show the alternating-bass pattern.

Assignment 37

Write a simple ballad using four lines to each verse. Your words should tell a story, preferably a moral tale. Use the C major scale for your tune. Keep the melody simple and unsyncopated. Use an alternating-bass accompaniment and the chord and verse structure shown below:

Line 1 $\frac{3}{4}$ | / / / | / / / | / / / | / / / |
         | C(I) | C | C | C |

Line 2 | / / / | / / / | / / / | / / / |
         | C | C | G(V) | G |

Line 3 | / / / | / / / | / / / | / / / |
         | C(I) | C | F(IV) | F |

Line 4 | / / / | / / / | / / / | / / / |
         | C(I) | G(V) | C(I) | C |

'The Grand Ole Opry' is America's longest-running country music radio programme. (The word 'opry' comes from the classical music term 'opera'.) It started in 1927 and many country stars made their names on the programme. At the beginning of the 1970s the programme was moved into a new multi-million-dollar complex of its own known as Opryland. Now hundreds of radio stations in the Southern States play nothing except country music round the clock. Among country music's stars are (or were) Hank Williams, Jim Reeves, Johnny Cash, Tammy Wynette, John Denver, Glenn Campbell, Kris Kristofferson, Roger Miller, Emmylou Harris, Dolly Parton and Tennessee Ernie Ford.

Music to hear

Folk: *Selections*, Martin Carthy, Pegasus PEG6.
Byker Hill, Martin Carthy, Topic 12TS 342.
American Folk Music, Vols. 1, 2 and 3, Folkways FP 251/2.

Bluegrass: *Bluegrass Favourites*, Crown CST 346.

Country and western: *Original Golden Hits*, Vols. 1 and 2, Johnny Cash, Sun 6467 001, 6467 007.
Me and Bobby McGee, Kris Kristofferson, Monument UK 64631.
20 Originals from the Country and Western Hall of Fame, Pickwick PLE 7006.

5 Don't Step On My Blue Suede Shoes: From rock'n'roll to teenage pop

ROCK'N'ROLL

When it began in 1954, **rock'n'roll** was a total shock, an explosion of power, an outrage – and yet it was a predictable development. America, and indeed the western world, was in a hopeful mood in the 1950s. World War II was over. For the first time 'teenagers' (the word was invented in the fifties) had money to spend and began searching for an identity as a group, for something to base their fashions on, something that was 'theirs', something exciting. Rock'n'roll was it!

Rock'n'roll was special because it was the bringing together of the many different threads of popular music. It rose to its greatest popularity in 1955–6 but there had been music with many of the rock'n'roll ingredients for some time before that.

The musical roots of rock'n'roll

Western swing bands of the 1940s began to use the boogie-woogie rhythm and by 1950 several country singers had put out records based on a boogie-woogie beat. These included 'Freight Train Boogie', 'Milkbucket Boogie', 'Hootowl Boogie' and 'Hobo Boogie' recorded by Red Foley (*Tennessee Saturday Night*, Charley Records, CR 30230). This country-boogie rhythm can be heard in songs like Bill Haley's 'Shake, Rattle and Roll', issued in 1954.

It is a short step from using the boogie-woogie rhythm to using the 12-bar blues. Listen to the verse form of 'Shake, Rattle and Roll' (the song can be found on Bill Haley's *Golden Hits* album, CBS MCL 1778); it has three lines, 12 bars and uses chords I, IV and V in the traditional blues sequence. Nevertheless, the instrumental sound, the lyrics and the style have been 'countrified'.

The guitar sound is clean, not distorted as in T-Bone Walker's city blues style (see page 29). The words are not as explicitly sexual as they were in the original blues on which this was loosely based. The melody in the key of C uses the notes C, E, G, A, and avoids blue-note effects. Perhaps this is why, successful as he was with teenagers in America and Europe, Bill Haley was never as popular as Elvis Presley. By comparison, Haley was too safe, too white in his musical influence. His country-style rock'n'roll came to be called 'rockabilly'. Its stars included country singers Johnny Cash, Carl Perkins, Roy Orbison and Gene Vincent.

Presley started out by singing country and rockabilly, but his career took off when he started to sing in a slurred 'bluesy' style. Before long, Presley was using the 'dirty' guitar sound of T-Bone Walker in the accompaniment to his songs and was not only singing aggressive and sexual lyrics but was also strutting and 'hip-grinding' on stage like a raw Chicago bluesman. Whereas white teenagers, particularly girls, could not have taken this raw sexuality from a black singer, Presley was white and therefore 'safe', but exciting as a fantasy figure.

Assignment 38

Listen carefully to the rock'n'roll songs listed below. List the white and black elements in each of them. You should include blues structure, scale, lyrics, 'clean' or 'dirty' guitar sounds and anything else that seems appropriate.

Bill Haley: 'Rock Around the Clock', 'See You Later Alligator' (*Golden Hits*, MCA MCF 2555)

Elvis Presley: 'Heartbreak Hotel', 'Blue Suede Shoes', 'Hound Dog' (*Greatest Hits*, Vol. 1, RCA NL 89024).

Saxophones were frequently used in rock'n'roll. The saxophone came from the city blues line-up and Bill Haley used it to play syncopated riffs (see page 22) behind the singer. In 'See You Later Alligator' the saxophone plays a simple riff after each line of singing. This idea of a line of singing and then a line of instrumental is a version of the 'call-and-response' patterning (see page 4) that is found in work-songs, spirituals and blues. In the Haley version the singer calls and the saxophone responds, but the response doesn't need to be an instrumental one. On his classic rock'n'roll hit 'What I'd Say', Ray Charles gives the call and the response is given in harmony by a group of backing vocalists in pure gospel style but with very secular lyrics.

Assignment 39

Using the accompaniment for a 12-bar blues (see page 14), compose a call-and-response song. There should be a call and a response for each of the three lines. The words can be very simple. The aim is to create an exciting effect.

THE CHUCK BERRY INFLUENCE

One of the first black rock'n'rollers to achieve success nationally was Chuck Berry. It was Berry who gave rock'n'roll a lot of its 'teenage' lyrics. He sang with style and humour about the things teenagers were interested in, and for the first time created a music that was all theirs. He sang about 'riding along in automobiles' with 'baby beside me at the wheel', about young love, drive-in movies, dressing just right, having fun. His list as a songwriter includes

Chuck Berry in the 1950s. His first record Maybellene *won the Billboard Triple Award for the rhythm'n'blues record selling most copies and getting the most playings on radio and jukebox.*

A more mature Chuck Berry does the 'duck walk'. Berry wrote such R'n'B standards as Roll Over Beethoven *and* Memphis Tennessee.

classics like 'Route 66', 'Bye Bye Johnny', 'Nadine', 'Sweet Little Sixteen', 'Johnny B. Goode', 'Roll Over Beethoven' and 'Memphis Tennessee'.

But Berry gave rock'n'roll something more than great songs; he gave a new style and force to rock guitar, both lead and rhythm. He played solos using the blues scale (see page 13) and playing double notes with a 'dirty' tone on the guitar, 'bending' notes (playing slightly below pitch) and repeating short riffs.

Assignment 40

Listen out for 'dirty' tones, bent notes and repeated riffs in a Chuck Berry guitar solo such as 'Sweet Little Sixteen' (PRT flashback reissue FDS 18).

Chuck Berry's 'bluesy' rhythm-guitar playing has been a big influence right up to the present day. What Berry did was to play hard-hitting chord-patterns on the bass strings of the guitar to create an even, but powerful, piano-boogie style. Here is a distinctive pattern for the chord of C:

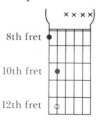

Assignment 41

(a) Learn how to play this riff on guitar (or keyboard). Deaden the guitar strings with your hands so that the notes are clipped and separate and sharply accent the first quaver of each pair.

(b) Transpose the Berry rhythm part to fit the chords of F, G, A, D, E. On the guitar this is easy. Just slide the shape about until your bass note, on the bottom E string, is the bass note of the chord.

(c) Fit this accompaniment to a 12-bar chord sequence. Listen to Chuck Berry singing 'Carol', 'Johnny B. Goode' or 'Route 66' (all these songs can be found on *Spotlight on Chuck Berry*, PRT SPOT 1003). Copy out the words to any one verse you choose and sing them over your accompaniment.

When rock'n'roll first came to a mass audience in 1955 the reaction was incredible and hysterical. Rock'n'roll stars were screamed at and mobbed. Parents thought the music was corrupting their children. Campaigns against rock'n'roll appeared on television. Preachers taught that rock'n'roll was evil.

Then a series of catastrophes brought rock'n'roll to an abrupt end. In the space of two years, all rock'n'roll's top men were put out of action. In 1957, Little Richard, who had had hits like 'Long Tall Sally', 'Lucille' and 'Tutti Frutti', left rock'n'roll to become an evangelist and sing gospel. In 1958, Elvis Presley entered the army, and in the same year a scandal broke out over the marriage of Jerry Lee Lewis to a minor. Chuck Berry was imprisoned for infringements of the immigration laws, and Buddy Holly, the Big Bopper

Jerry Lee Lewis, one of the authentic rock'n'rollers.

and Ritchie Valens were all killed in a plane crash, in 1959. That same year a national scandal broke when Alan Freed, the disc jockey who had largely sold rock'n'roll to America, was found guilty of accepting bribes to play certain records. The record companies and radio stations wanted something safer and more respectable, and so, from 1958-63, we had the age of the 'teen idol'.

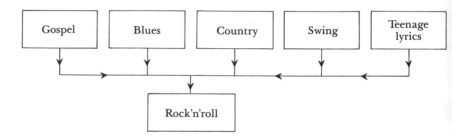

TEENAGE POP

There were two strands in response to this desire for a 'cleaner' less 'dangerous' popular music. A new sound emerged on the west coast of America embodying the clean, healthy (and well-off) image of the west-coast American teenager. The 'surfing scene' was about having FUN, particularly during the long semester vacations spent at the beach. Among the pioneers of this sound were Jan and Dean, whose complex multi-tracked vocals were first painstakingly recorded on home hi-fi and culminated in 1963 with the remarkable 'Surf City' (CR204). Also emerging at this time were The Beach Boys who developed the sound throughout the sixties with songs like 'Fun, Fun, Fun' and 'Good Vibrations' (CL16054).

Assignment 42

Listen to The Beach Boys' 'Good Vibrations' on their *Smiley Smile* album (ST9001), paying particular attention to the use of multi-track vocals and other studio effects.

Meanwhile, the record companies had recognised the potential of 'teenage romance' and the 'teen idol' particularly with the large record-buying group of girls in their mid-teens. Record companies realised that if they could control teenage tastes they could control the market and the profits. The idea was to decide on a look and a sound, choose a safe, respectable, good-looking teenager to fit both, get a team of songwriters to produce a song about 'teenage concerns' and make a record. They then could sell the record on radio and television shows with the right packaging, and a hit was virtually guaranteed. This highly successful approach produced hits like 'Puppy Love' by Paul Anka (*The Original Hits*, CBS 32380); 'Sealed with a Kiss' by Brian Hyland (Old Gold reissue, OG 9174); 'Hey Paula!' by Paul and Paula (OG 9099). This music was, on the whole, less innovative and ambitious than what was going on on the west coast, but the message contained in the lyrics was thought to be as basic to teenage life as having fun: falling in LOVE.

Hit factories

Many very talented songwriters were recruited into hit-making 'factories' by the record companies and expected to mass-produce songs. One of these 'hit-factories' was the Brill Building in New York's Tin Pan Alley, which housed songwriters like Gerry Goffin, Carole King, Barry Mann, Cynthia

Weil, Neil Diamond, Howard Greenfield and Neil Sedaka. They usually worked in pairs with a piano, in tiny cubicles. They turned out hits like 'Will You Love Me Tomorrow?', 'Take Good Care of My Baby', 'Crying in the Rain', 'The Loco-motion', 'It Might As Well Rain Until September', 'I Love How You Love Me', 'Walking in the Rain', 'You've Lost that Loving Feeling', 'Stupid Cupid', 'Oh Carol', 'Happy Birthday Sweet Sixteen' and 'Breaking Up is Hard to Do'.

One common musical feature of this pop music was the use of a major scale and chords I, IV, V and VI. Sometimes these chords were put in the order I-VI-IV-V which was repeated two or three times with a different sequence like I-IV-I-V to finish off the verse. In the key of C major the I-VI-IV-V sequence is C, A minor, F, G. Songs would end with a return to chord I: I-VI-IV-V-I, or I-IV-I-V-I.

Assignment 43   Write out the names of the chords in the I–VI–IV–V sequence in the keys of D major, G major and A major.

These chords were often played in *arpeggio* style (each note played separately) on a dull-sounding echoed guitar, or oozed out on syrupy strings. Here is the arpeggio for the chord of C:

C   E   G   C   G   E
Count ①   2   3   ②   2   3

Assignment 44   (a)   Work out the arpeggios for the other chords in the I–VI–IV–V sequence in the key of C.

(b)   Do the same for the keys of D major, G major and A major, and learn to play the sequence on the instrument of your choice in all three keys.

Assignment 45   (a)   Now record an arpeggio backing for the following sequence:

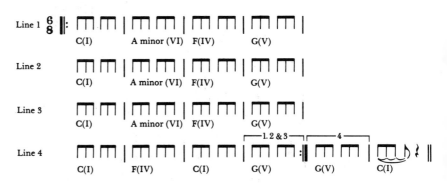

(b)   When you have recorded your backing, write a tune to fit it in the key of C major. Your first two, or even three, lines can be the same if you wish.

(c)   Put words to your tune. They should be about breaking up with your boyfriend or girlfriend.

One style of backing was for a group of vocalists to 'ooh' or 'aah' or 'bop bop bop bop' in time with the chord sequence. This *vocal-harmony* approach was a descendant of gospel, choral singing and of vocal group jazz, which was quite popular during the 1940s. Sometimes rather than sing background 'oohs' the whole group would sing the lyrics and harmonize the tune. 'Lollipop' by The Chordettes is a classic example of this.

Teenage pop was fun at times but it lacked the earthy drive which had made rock'n'roll so exciting.

Music to hear

Rock'n'roll: *The Roots of Rock'n'roll*, Savoy 2221.
The Jerry Lee Lewis Collection, Pickwick PDA007.
22 Original Hits, Little Richard, Warwick WW5034.
What I'd Say, Ray Charles, Atlantic K40029.
40 Greatest Hits, Elvis Presley, RCA PL42691.
Elvis Presley Collection, Pickwick PDA 042.
Greatest Hits, Chuck Berry Marble Arch UK MAL 660.
Golden Hits, Chuck Berry, Mercury 61103.

Teenage pop: *Lemon Popsicle*, Warwick WW5050.
Very Best of Bobby Vee, Sunset SLS 50271.
Writer, Carole King, A&M AMLS 996.

Rockabilly: *Golden Hits*, Bill Haley, MCA MCF 2555.

6 Money (That's What I Want): Black musicians gain commercial status

Until the 1950s, the story of popular music had mainly been about how white artists had gained commercial success by copying and blending black music with their own. Now black artists began mixing their music with that of the whites and gradually came to gain equal commercial status, although it was not until well into the 1960s that this process was complete.

RHYTHM'N'BLUES

In the 1950s, completely within the black or 'race record' market, gospel singers like Sam Cooke had been mixing their gospel style with city-blues instrumentation. The vocal-harmony and singing style were pure gospel, but the rhythms were a blues and gospel mix and the lyrics were close to sexually explicit blues. Songs like 'Have Mercy Baby' by the Dominoes, had changed 'Lord' to 'Baby' and the song had shifted the object of passion from God to woman. **Rhythm'n'blues** or R'n'B was born. Its best-known group is the Drifters.

DOO-WOP

During the late 1950s another style of vocal-harmony sound emerged which came to be called **doo-wop**, after the nonsense syllables sung by the backing vocalists. Doo-wop was a cross between the ballads of black, vocal-jazz groups, like The Ink Spots, and R'n'B. The lead vocalist was featured more prominently and the sound of doo-wop was cleaner and more relaxed than R'n'B. It also owed a lot to the style of production of the rock'n'roll and teenage-pop records of the time.

Two black groups, the Platters and the Coasters, had a string of pop hits in this style. Among these hits were 'Only You', 'The Great Pretender' and 'Smoke Gets in Your Eyes' by the Platters, and 'Searchin'', 'Yakety Yak', 'Charlie Brown', 'Along Came Jones' and 'Poison Ivy', by the Coasters, whose material was written by the up-market Jerry Leiber and Mike Stoller.

Leiber and Stoller moved on to write for a group called the Drifters, and with them the black vocal-group sound began to shape up ready for the great soul and Tamla Motown explosion of the 1960s. The Drifters had a string of classic hits including 'The Last Dance for Me', 'Sweets for my Sweet', 'Under the Boardwalk', 'Saturday Night at the Movies' and 'Come on Over to My Place'.

THE SPECTOR SOUND

Another element in the black vocal-group sound was added by white songwriter/producer Phil Spector. Spector wrote catchy pop songs but his arrangements and the production (the overall sound) on his records were unique. He used studio techniques to multi-track (record separately, then play back together) instruments, vocals and rhythm parts. He also made use of a wide-range of instruments: strings, timpani, and brass were all multi-tracked to create a gigantic wall of sound. Most of all he built up a very powerful backbeat (accents on off-beats).

Doo-wop stars, the Coasters.

The Ronettes, stars from the Phil Spector stable.

Spector hits included: 'He's Sure the Boy I Love', 'Da doo ron ron', 'Then he Kissed Me', by the Crystals; 'Be my Baby', 'Baby I Love You', 'Breakin' Up', 'Walking in the Rain', by the Ronettes; 'River Deep and Mountain High', by Ike and Tina Turner and 'You've Lost that Loving Feeling', by the Righteous Brothers.

Assignment 46

(a) Write a simple melody, five to eight notes long. Practise this melody, playing it together in a group on whatever instruments are at hand. Record it on tape. Listen to the tape and then play the melody again, keeping in time with the recorded melody. When you can co-ordinate the tape and the live instruments turn up the volume of the tape recorder so that the recorded and live sounds are at the same level. Now record both kinds of sound onto another tape on a second tape recorder. Then play live with this second tape and record back onto the first. Do this two or three times, and see how 'meaty' a sound you can produce by multi-tracking in this way.

(b) Repeat the previous exercise playing a chord instead of a tune. You should 'spread' your instruments so that no two are playing the same note at the same octave. After multi-tracking you should have a really thick chord-sound.

(c) Multi-track the accompaniment to the song you wrote in assignment 45, or to any well-known pop song from the period 1958-62. Get some of the instruments to build up full, sustained chords using single chords; get other instruments to play arpeggios. Arrange your percussion instruments so that the off-beats are emphasised (beat 2 in $\frac{6}{8}$; beats 2 and 4 in $\frac{4}{4}$) to give the 'backbeat' feel.

(d) When you come to play back the accompaniment sing your tune along with it and get everybody to clap loudly on the beats emphasised by the percussion instruments.

TAMLA MOTOWN

The next step for this gospel-and-pop mix came when Berry Gordy set up Tamla Motown in 1960. Tamla Motown, based in Detroit, was an all-black record company: the management, artists, songwriters and producers were all black.

At Tamla Motown, the songwriter and vocal-group tradition was developed still further. The backbeat was important as were a lavish Spector-like recording sound and the doo-wop/gospel harmonies. The songs often had the slushy lyrics of late 1950s teenage pop, but in terms of melody, form and recording quality they had progressed a long way.

Tamla Motown's own songwriters, Holland–Dozier–Holland and Smokey Robinson, moved the popular song forward in revolutionary fashion. They did not stick to the four-line verse of country and western and much pop, or to the A A B A song form which had been popular since the days of swing. Instead they gave their songs structures like A B A B C C and pushed home the impact of their songs by repeating the title lines of their choruses (called 'hook-lines') over and over again, so that these hooks became unforgettable.

Assignment 47

(a) Listen to a few Tamla Motown records from the early 1960s and make a note of their structure. Alternatively you can work out the structures from the sheet music.

(b) Write down lyrics of the hook-line for each song and count how many times it occurs.

(c) For each song, write down one sentence which sums up the theme of the song.

Assignment 48

Write your own tune with an A B A B C C structure. Give the song a repeated hook-line. Use chords I, IV, V and VI in any order, and in the key of C major.

Tamla Motown also had its own studio musicians who played on the records of all Tamla Motown artists. Before long they developed a distinctive sound with a loud, punchy, syncopated bass-line. Often, an orchestra was used to fill out the sound.

The whole Tamla Motown machine was smooth running and guaranteed to make hits. In 1966, 75% of its singles made the charts. On stage, Tamla Motown artists wore suits or sequined dresses as a 'uniform' and precision dance-steps were worked out for each number. For above all, Tamla Motown produced excellent dance music.

The list of Tamla Motown hits is enormous, with many black artists owing their success to promotion by the company. Such artists have included Martha and the Vandellas, The Temptations, Marvin Gaye, Smokey Robinson, Stevie Wonder, The Supremes, The Four Tops, Gladys Knight and the Pips, and The Jackson Five.

Martha and the Vandellas and
Marvin Gaye, exponents of the
Tamla Motown sound.

SOUL MUSIC

Tamla Motown is usually thought of as 'soul' music, but the heart of soul music was really Stax records, closely linked with Atlantic records and based in Memphis. Stax came straight from the R'n'B tradition. It had strong links with gospel based on the rock'n'roll of Ray Charles. Compared to Tamla Motown, songs recorded on Stax sounded raw, rough and edgy, and the accompaniment usually consisted only of guitar, bass, drums, organ and brass section. Stax songs were much simpler and less melodic than Tamla Motown songs, much closer to blues and gospel; they stuck to a handful of chords and didn't repeat the hook line so often or so forcefully. Stax singers often improvised around the tune in wild, gospel style and the songs were often sexual in tone, or else concerned about passionate love and heartbreak, dancing and having a good time.

'Mustang Sally' by Wilson Pickett is a classic example of Stax. Listen to it. The song takes the form of a blues.

Assignment 49

Write down a bar chart like the one for popular-song form on page 24, showing where the chords change during a verse of 'Mustang Sally' (available on *The Best of Wilson Pickett*, Atlantic K50750).

49

The accompaniment to 'Mustang Sally' is typical of Stax records. The backbeat is there, but is delayed in the second half of each bar, giving a jerky, hypnotic rhythm (which is a forerunner of the funk music of the late 1970s – see page 85).

Count 1   2 & a 3 & 4 &

Assignment 50

Tap out this rhythm, giving a heavy accent to the stressed notes.

The guitar plays a variation of the Chuck Berry guitar bass-chords (see page 40) over this rhythm while the brass section plays unison riffs made up of detached notes during the first two lines of the verse and long, sustained chords in the last line. The Stax session band which provided this backing was given much more freedom than the Motown one and earned its own international reputation under the name of Booker T. and the M.G.s.

Assignment 51

(a) Use either your own 12-bar blues tune or another well-known blues and put the Stax rhythm to it by using a drum kit, drum machine, taps and claps, etc. On piano or guitar get someone to play this variation of the Chuck Berry bass-chords:

(In C position)
Count   1 & 2 & 3 & 4 &   (1) & 2 & 3 & 4 &

(b) Sing the tune but 'chop up' the way you sing to give a kind of percussive effect. This is, in effect, improvising by changing the length of notes. If you can also add an instrumental 'response' to the 'call' of the vocal line by way of a short, snappy riff, so much the better.

Wilson Pickett characterizes the rough, raw sound of Stax records.

Sometimes Stax artists began a live performance in a suit, like Motown singers, but the jacket and tie were soon discarded: Stax went for the extrovert solo performer, not the precision dance-step 'cool' of the Motown groups.

Among the stars of Stax/Atlantic soul were Eddie Floyd, Solomon Burke, Wilson Pickett, Percy Sledge, James Brown, Otis Redding and Aretha Franklin.

Assignment 52

Compare some of the above performers with some of the Motown performers listed on page 48. What are the differences in style?

Music to hear

R'n'B:	*This is Sam Cooke*, RCA UK 2007.
Doo-wop:	*20 Great Originals*, The Coasters, Atlantic K30057.
	24 Original Hits, The Drifters, Atlantic K60106.
Spector:	*Sing their Greatest Hits*, The Ronettes, Phil Spector 2307 003.
	Greatest Hits, The Crystals, Philles 4003.
	River Deep and Mountain High, Ike and Tina Turner, A&M P8013.
Tamla Motown:	*Greatest Hits*, The Supremes, Tamla STML 11256.
	Greatest Hits, Marvin Gaye, Tamla STML 11153.
	Greatest Hits, Stevie Wonder, Tamla STML 11196.
Atlantic Soul:	*This is Soul*, Atlantic K20023.
	Best of Wilson Pickett, Atlantic K40015.
	The Best of Otis Redding, Atlantic K60016.
	The Best of James Brown, Polydor 2343 036.
	The World of Aretha Franklin, Columbia 31355.

7 (I Can't Get No) Satisfaction: From the Beatles to The Who

BEAT MUSIC

When the Beatles burst into the charts in 1963 they seemed so fresh, so new, so different. Nobody had seen or heard anything like them and their music before. But, looking back, we can see that their music was the product of a multitude of influences.

The Beatles came from Liverpool, a sea-port like New Orleans, which had its own musical traditions in the form of music-hall and folk songs, as well as a large Irish population with its own music. Besides this, sailors would bring back from America 'race records' and teenage pop which could not easily be bought elsewhere in Britain. Many Liverpool groups started off, during the 1950s, playing black and white American folk music on guitars, string bass, snare drums and washboard (this was known as **skiffle** and was popularized in Britain by Lonnie Donegan) and then played rock'n'roll, R'n'B, Motown, soul, gospel, blues and folk. Some had also played in clubs in the red-light district of Hamburg, a German sea-port, and elsewhere in Europe. There they had to play for hours on end, day and night, and would perform any songs they could think of to fill in the time.

When the Beatles finally got a recording contract and appeared on television to promote their second single 'Please Please Me', it was obvious that popular music had changed again. All four members of the band – John Lennon, Paul McCartney, Ringo Starr and George Harrison – wore a strange, new, 'long' haircut. They wore collarless French jackets, and the latest style of trousers, shirts and shoes. They had charm, personality and presented a new image.

The Beatles' music itself sounded so fresh because it was a new mixture of black and white styles. If you listen to songs from the first of the Beatles' albums you'll easily be able to tell where the music had its roots. There are songs in black R'n'B, Tamla Motown and rock'n'roll style as well as standard 'pop' songs. The three-part vocals which the Beatles used on many tracks were derived from the black vocal-group tradition, doo-wop, Spector and Motown. Even the songs written by Lennon and McCartney reflect both black and pop influences. 'There's a Place' is in the Goffin/King pop tradition. The verse form of 'Can't Buy Me Love' is a 12-bar blues. 'Eight Days a Week' is in the black-girl vocal-group tradition and is a reworking of the I–VI–IV–I chord sequence.

On later albums and singles the influences can still be heard:

Song	Influence
'Get Back'	Atlantic soul
'Lady Madonna'	Piano blues
'Let It Be'	Hymn
'Maxwell's Silver Hammer' 'When I'm Sixty-Four'	1920s dance-band music/Music-hall
'Taxman'	Tamla Motown
'Yellow Submarine'	Children's street songs
'Act Naturally'	Country and western

The Beatles' songs and arrangements blended all these elements, black and white, and came up with something new. And to begin with, the group

did all this just with vocals, electric and acoustic guitars and drums. Initially
their lyrics were straightforward pop, but these changed as the sixties
progressed.

When they had got over the initial shock of the Beatles' hairstyles, even the
mums and dads came to like them – which was the problem. Young people,
while still secretly liking the group, were soon looking around for something
else that parents would not like. Other beat groups did not fit the bill. Gerry
and the Pacemakers, the Searchers, and Billy J. Kramer and the Dakotas
were far too light and 'poppy', in style.

Assignment 53   Listen to songs on the *Please Please Me* (Parlophone PCS 3042) and *With
the Beatles* (Parlophone PCS 3045) albums, plus early hit singles by the
Searchers and Gerry and the Pacemakers. For each song pick out and list the
influences, and any of the musical effects, forms or techniques we have
covered so far.

No fancy suits for the Rolling Stones.

BRITISH R'N'B

The Rolling Stones - Mick Jagger, Keith Richard, Brian Jones, Bill Wyman and Charlie Watts - were outrageous enough to please many teenagers. The Stones wore their hair really long and scruffy. They didn't wear suits or a uniform on stage but instead dressed in the latest casual gear. Whereas beat came from Liverpool, British R'n'B was based in the London pubs and clubs.

The difference showed in the music too. Pop did not feature on Stones' albums. At first they played their own versions of Chuck Berry songs, city blues and soul. They drew from the raw end of black music while the Beatles chose the Tamla Motown style. Like the Beatles, the Stones adapted the material and added their own flavour and distinctive sound: Richards played a distorted Chuck Berry guitar; Jagger sang in a sullen, menacing soul/blues voice; Jones often used a blues slide guitar. The mix, or instrumental balance, on their records was muddy and thick. A comparison of the Stones' and Beatles' versions of 'I Wanna be Your Man' shows this clearly.

On stage the Stones were menacing and sexual, Jagger developing a tremendous stage strut and vacant stare which enraged adult audiences.

The Stones were quickly followed by other R'n'B bands like the Animals, the Pretty Things, and the Yardbirds, but none had the same thickness of sound coupled with the ability to shock.

Since the Beatles' arrival, groups had begun to write their own songs. In 1965, the Stones wrote and recorded 'Satisfaction', which was a massive hit in Britain and America. It paved the way for rock music (as opposed to rock'n'roll). 'Satisfaction' has all the elements of Atlantic soul but more besides. It has the soul beat. The guitars are distorted to sound like a brass section and play the riff that runs through much of the song. The song has several hook-lines; one step better than Motown. It is the lyrics which add something new. 'I can't get no "satisfaction"', is a double-meaning hook-line in the blues tradition, but the verse is the voice of a cynical young person ripping to shreds the commerciality of the packaged and advertised 'plastic' world he lives in:

> I'm watching my T.V. and a man comes on and tells me how white my shirt should be but he can't be a man 'cos he doesn't smoke the same cigarettes as me. I can't get no . . . no, no, no.

This was a radical departure from the love songs in the charts at that time, but in fact there was a tradition behind even this. The tradition, dating back to Woody Guthrie and before, was of the protest song being brought into the rock world by an American singer called Bob Dylan (see page 59). 'Satisfaction', with its blend of soul, blues-based instrumentation and aggressive lyrics, marked the end of British R'n'B and heralded the age of rock.

MOD MUSIC (1965)

The mods or 'modernists' were fashion-conscious early-1960s teenagers who favoured a smart look, even in casual clothes. Their fashions included moccasin shoes, sport shirts, 'pop-art' shirts and jumpers, and ex-army parkas. They rode motor scooters which had as many lights and mirrors as the owner could afford and which would fit on.

Mods were crazy about dancing. They held all-night dances and often stayed awake by taking amphetamine pills or 'uppers'. These were addictive and dangerous but gave the user artificial energy. Mods loved soul and Tamla Motown, but around 1965, mod groups appeared. These included the Small Faces and others, but the main group was The Who.

The Who have been through many musical phases and have given much to popular music on the way. They were in the third wave of British bands to be influenced by Tamla Motown and soul but Pete Townshend, their lead guitarist and songwriter, developed these musical roots in a radically new direction. Townshend's music, and The Who's style, were geared not to mod dances but to the crazy energy and aggression of the pill culture. Townshend used feedback (a loud whine developed by overamplifying the guitar) and ended the act by smashing his guitar on stage. It was a great display of teenage frustration. 'Anyway, Anyhow, Anywhere' displays many of these innovations.

Power chords

It was these powerful guitar chords which gave the final ingredient to the recipe for 'rock' music.

Mods.

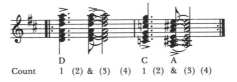

Here is an illustration of Townshend's chord-style:

Count   1   (2)   &   (3)   (4)   1   (2)   &   (3)   (4)

The sequence is of major chords based on the blue-note scale. Using a C major chord in the key of D is typical of folk style as it's in the Mixolydian mode (see page 32). The second beat of each bar comes earlier than expected. The chords are 'fat', using every note available from the instruments in a big spread, but this idea had been used by the brass sections of swing bands, and by Spector multi-tracking. What made The Who's sound original was that the group did these things with such volume and attack using electric guitars. The effect was one of great force.

Assignment 54

[cassette icon]

If you have an electric guitar and amplifier, try this experiment: Turn the controls on the guitar and amplifier up full, hold down a chord, or just leave the strings open; do not strum but just hold the guitar near the amplifier. You should get deafening feedback. Turn the guitar's tone switches or flick the selector switches and see what effects you get.

Many people say that Townshend wrote the ultimate rock song: 'My Generation'. Listen to the teenage theme, the frustrated stutter, the aggression, the crazy instrumental solo, the chaotic drumming. The Who had other hits. They were also the first band to have a successful rock opera, *Tommy*, but their lasting contribution to music comes from this early style and energy.

Music to hear

Beat music: *Please Please Me*, The Beatles, Parlophone PCS 3042.
                      Beatles For Sale, Parlophone PCS 3062.
                      1962–66, The Beatles, Parlophone PCSP 717.

British R'n'B: *The Rolling Stones*, Decca LK 4605.
                      The Rolling Stones 2, Decca SLK 4661.
                      Rolling Stones EP, Decca DFE 8560.
                      Best of The Animals, ABCKO AB 4226.

Mod music: *My Generation*, The Who, Virgin UK V2179.

Rock music: *Who's Next*, The Who, Track 2408 102.
                      Let It Bleed, The Rolling Stones Decca SKL 5025.

8 Cosmic Wheels: The 1960s

The 1960s were a time of social unrest, a dramatic time. The Cuban missile crisis brought the world to the brink of nuclear war. President J.F. Kennedy and Senator Robert Kennedy were assassinated. The black people of America and Catholics in Northern Ireland marched for civil rights. Black leader Martin Luther King was murdered and the Black Power movement began. America was fighting a war in Vietnam which became increasingly unpopular with young people and resulted in huge anti-war marches, riots by the police in Chicago, sit-ins and the occupation of universities by students. There were riots in Paris; Russia invaded Czechoslovakia; the Cultural Revolution was under way in China.

PROTEST MUSIC

Young people were shocked by the injustice in the world and, often in a naïve way, tried to stop it. The music of the time could not help but reflect this attempt.

The Vietnam war created an enormous anti-war movement in America and stimulated a whole new generation of protest singers following in the tradition of Woody Guthrie.

There was a tradition of social protest in folk music dating back to Woody Guthrie (see page 33) and in the early 1960s this movement gained strength through people like Pete Seeger, Joan Baez and, especially, Bob Dylan. To begin with Dylan sang his songs to his own guitar accompaniment. His lyrics had real venom:

Come you masters of war
You that build all the guns
You that build the death planes
You that build the big bombs
You that hide behind walls
You that hide behind desks
I just want you to know
I can see through your masks.

You that never done nothin'
But build to destroy
You play with my world
Like it's your little toy
You put a gun in my hand
And you hide from my eyes
And you turn and run farther
When the fast bullets fly.

You fasten the triggers
For others to fire
Then you sit back and watch
When the death count gets higher
You hide in your mansion
As young people's blood
Flows out of their bodies
And is buried in the mud.

Verses from 'Masters Of War' by Bob Dylan

'Masters Of War' was set to the tune of a traditional English folk song called 'Nottamun Town'. There are many recordings of the original tune. Listen to the version by Fairport Convention on their LP *What We Did on Our Holidays* (Island ILPS 9092). Many of the early Dylan songs were traditional folk songs, country numbers or blues, all with Dylan's own words.

Assignment 55 Select a folk song, or a country and western number. Choose a topic you feel strongly about – like racial prejudice, unemployment, war, nuclear weapons, starvation, or any other social theme, and write your own words on this topic to fit the original melody.

Assignment 56 Write a song of your own in folk style, using either a major key or one of the folk modes (see page 32). Put your own protest lyrics to it.

Dylan was much more than just a folk protest singer. By 1965, the themes and lyrics of his most influential numbers, such as 'Like a Rolling Stone', were personal as well as social.

Assignment 57

Listen to 'Like a Rolling Stone' (Bob Dylan's *Greatest Hits*, CBS 62847). What is the song about? Is it a protest song about injustice, or a revenge song about an ex-girlfriend? What do we learn about the characters in the song and about the society in which they live?

FOLK-ROCK

Dylan lost a lot of his folk audience when he began to play with a rock band, although he gained the larger rock market. The music was still a version of simple folk or blues themes but the rock band changed the whole effect.

Assignment 58

Listen to some of Dylan's lyrics from his albums *Bringing It All Back Home*, *Highway 61 Revisited*, and *Blonde on Blonde* (details of these albums can be found at the end of this chapter). Pick one song and try to explain what it is about.

Dylan's move to rock had changed what could be done with folk and rock songs. In 1965 the Beatles were releasing albums like *Help* which were still basically about love, boy meets girl, boy loses girl, boy gets girl back. Dylan was releasing peculiar musical poetry with songs often ten minutes in length. Rock began to follow this trend.

Bob Dylan started as a protest singer but later moved to a rock-style band and more personal lyrics.

PSYCHEDELIC ROCK

The other major influences on music at this time were not themselves musical. One was the drug LSD which was becoming a regular part of the rock scene. LSD is very powerful; it creates believable pictures, or hallucinations, for the user and distorts his or her sense of time, touch, smell, taste, hearing and reasoning. For some users the drug was a revelation. For others it was a disaster. It changed musicians' perception of sound, and it changed what they wanted to say and how they wanted to say it. In 1966, the Beatles' *Revolver* album reflected this change. The lyrics throughout the album were often weird; the last track, 'Tomorrow Never Knows', featured an Indian sitar and was totally different from anything which had gone before. It was 'psychedelic'. **Psychedelic rock** was the name given to music which attempted to re-create or portray, by means of words and sounds, the LSD drug experience.

On 'Tomorrow never knows' hardly one single instrument could be distinguished, since they had been distorted, taped and played backwards, and echoed. This was made possible through the great advances in recording technology. The same technology produced various electronic effects boxes which altered the sound of instruments on stage, such as *fuzz* (a strong distortion), *wah-wah* (the effect is like the name), *overdrive* (artificial feedback), *flanger* (a metallic doubling up of sound) and *echo*. These effects fitted the psychedelic or drug scene very well because of their weird quality. In the next three or four years new instruments like the mellotron and the electronic synthesiser appeared, which made it possible to create new instrumental sounds.

Hippies at the Rolling Stones concert in Hyde Park in 1967.

Assignment 59   Carry out the following sound experiments:

(a)   Play back a 45rpm record at slow speed (i.e. 33⅓rpm) with all the bass turned off on the amplifier.

(b)   Record your own music on a reel-to-reel tape recorder and play it back at the wrong speed.

(c)   Record a common, everyday sound – like crinkling newspaper – close to the microphone and then play it back at the wrong speed. You can do the same with sounds recorded outside like cars, aeroplanes, people talking, or with musical instruments, singing, stamping, clapping, laughing and so on.

(Richard Orton's *Electronic music for schools* (Cambridge University Press, 1981), contains other interesting ideas for experimenting with sound.)

GUITAR HEROES

With the new electronic effects, the guitarist really came into his own. Following the 1964 R'n'B boom there had been a brief revival of interest in the blues, particularly in Britain. From blues groups like John Mayall's Bluesbreakers and the Yardbirds (who soon moved into psychedelic music) came a generation of fine guitarists like Peter Green (who formed Fleetwood Mac), Mick Taylor (who joined The Rolling Stones) and Jimmy Page (who went from the Yardbirds to create Led Zeppelin).

One of the best-known guitar heroes is Eric Clapton. Clapton went from Mayall to form the first supergroup, called Cream, with bass player Jack Bruce and drummer Ginger Baker. On record, they performed psychedelic rock using all the latest sounds and techniques and sang some very strange material. On stage, they would perform the first verse of a number, improvise over the verse chord-structure using the blues scale, sometimes for as long as half-an-hour and then return to the song for another verse to conclude. Soon many bands featured long instrumental breaks.

Fan poster of guitar hero Jimi Hendrix.

Assignment 60

Write a riff using the blues scale in C, with its E♭ and B♭. Repeat the riff for two minutes on tape. Play it back and improvise over it using the blues scale.

Perhaps the most accomplished of all the guitarists ever produced in popular music was Jimi Hendrix. After discovering him in a New York club, manager Chas Chandler brought Hendrix to Britain and set him up with his own group, the Jimi Hendrix Experience. Even today, guitarists can't imagine how he produced many of his sounds and effects using only a guitar. He could play brilliantly in most styles and moods. He played his guitar behind his head, from the wrong side of the neck, and with his teeth. At the Woodstock festival he played the American National anthem in protest against the Vietnam War, re-creating in the middle, just with the guitar, the sound of an American air attack on a Vietnamese village.

THE LOVE CULTURE

Festivals were another feature of the late 1960s. Eastern and mystical religions and philosophies were all the rage with the 'hippies', or 'flower children'. Teenagers were wearing beads, kaftans, bell-bottoms and sandals, trying out free love and going on anti-war marches. The Beatles went to India to study under a guru, the Maharishi Mahesh Yogi. Their song summing all this up, 'All You Need is Love', was beamed live to the whole world by satellite. It seemed as though rock music was going to change everything. The climax of all this was the Woodstock festival 'three days of love and peace', which had one of the biggest line-ups of rock talent ever.

But there was a dangerous undercurrent to the sixties. The Rolling Stones were singing songs like 'Street Fighting Man', 'Let It Bleed', 'Sympathy for the Devil', and 'Midnight Rambler'. Drugs were beginning to take their toll. The stars were getting too big, the scene was getting too selfish. There were Hell's Angels as well as hippies.

Hells Angels 'supervise' security at the Rolling Stones concert at Altamont, California in 1969.

After the excitement of Woodstock came the festival at Altamont in California, where the Stones hired Hell's Angels to do the security and part of the payment was in alcohol. There was impure LSD circulating at the festival and during the Stones' act the Angels killed a member of the audience with knives and pool cues.

Several leading rock stars died of drugs and drink around 1970, including Janis Joplin, Jim Morrison and Jimi Hendrix. After breaking his neck in a motorcycling accident, Bob Dylan returned to sing country and western. Finally, the Beatles split up amid lawsuits and money squabbles. The revolutionary dreams of the sixties were over. Popular music had, once again, suddenly lost many of its leading figures.

Assignment 61   Listen to one song from each of these influential albums of the 1960s (details on page 66: *Sergeant Pepper's Lonely Hearts Club Band* by the Beatles; *Let It Bleed* by The Rolling Stones; *Piper At The Gates Of Dawn* by Pink Floyd; *Disraeli Gears* by Cream; *Are You Experienced?* by the Jimi Hendrix Experience. List the distinctively sixties elements in each: for example, recording tricks, electronic effects, blues-based guitar solos, protest lyrics, love and peace lyrics, religious lyrics, Indian instruments and sounds.

Assignment 62   Compose and record a song with a strange fairy-story or magical lyrics. Play the backing fast, record it and play it back at a slower speed. Sing over this slow backing while recording both on another tape recorder. Try to incorporate one of the following sequences of notes or chords featuring a bass which descends by step. These were popular in this period especially with the Beatles. Use $\frac{3}{4}$ or $\frac{4}{4}$ time.

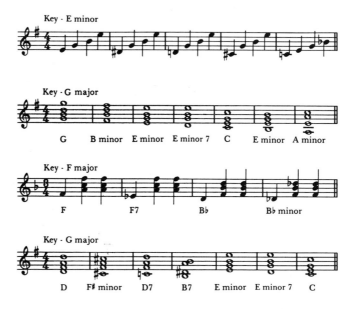

Assignment 63   You can tell from the examples in Assignment 62 how complicated the chord structures of pop songs had become, compared with what had gone before. Listen to 'I Want You (She's So Heavy)' from the Beatles' *Abbey Road* album. Play the chorus, shown below, as a group or by multi-tracking.

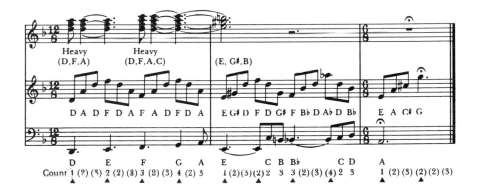

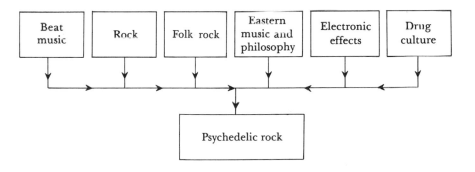

Music to hear

Protest music: *Freewheelin' Bob Dylan*, CBS 8786.

Times They Are A-Changing, Bob Dylan, CBS 8905.

Folk-rock: *Bringing It All Back Home*, Bob Dylan, CBS 9128.

Highway 61 Revisited, Bob Dylan, CBS 9189.

Blonde on Blonde, Bob Dylan, CBS C25841.

Psychedelic rock: *Revolver*, The Beatles, Parlophone PGS 7009.

Sergeant Pepper's Lonely Hearts Club Band, The Beatles, Parlophone PGS 7027.

Piper at The Gates Of Dawn, Pink Floyd, Columbia SCX 6157.

Meddle, Pink Floyd, Harvest SHVL 795.

Disraeli Gears, Cream, Polydor 2442 114.

Wheels Of Fire, Cream, Polydor 2612 001.

Are You Experienced?, Jimi Hendrix, Backtrack 2407 010.

Electric Ladyland, Jimi Hendrix, Polydor 2657 012.

Let It Bleed, The Rolling Stones, Decca SKL 5025.

9 Anarchy In the U.K.:
From heavy rock to punk

In the early 1970s pop started to splinter into different styles, each with its own loyal audience, each developing the themes of the 1960s in different ways. One thing many of the styles shared was a sense of extravagance, with fans idolising their heroes. Rock concerts became large scale, showy occasions held in huge concert halls, arenas or sports stadiums. Ticket prices shot up. The shows became increasingly spectacular; the artist or band wore outrageously flashy costumes; the light shows became ever more colourful and dazzling. There seemed no limit to rock's sense of its own importance.

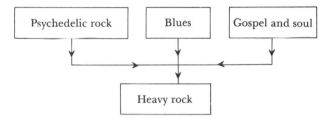

Elton John in plain clothes!

HEAVY ROCK

Heavy rock is a high energy music. It is based on the image of the guitar hero and has its roots in blues guitar and blues scales. The kind of guitar riff used by Clapton and Hendrix was developed, and sometimes speeded up, to form the basis of most songs.

Here is an example from 'Black Dog', a song from Led Zeppelin's fourth album:

	E	G G♯ A E		C	A		D E C D C		A A	C		A	G A		A D E C	D A
Count (1)(2)&	3 & 4 &		1	2		3 &	4 & a	1 &	2		3	4 &		1 & 2 &	3 &	(4)

Assignment 64 Learn to play the riff from 'Black Dog'.

Another feature of heavy rock was that the riff itself was usually played by both lead guitar and bass.

Heavy rock also developed the crashing, syncopated guitar chords of guitarists like Pete Townshend. Here is an example from the same number:

Chord name	C	A		A G A	C	A		A G A	C	A	G		D		A G A
Note value	♩	♩.	♪♪ ♩	♩ ♩.	♪♪♪	♩ ♩.	♩.	♪♩. ♩	♪♪
Count	1	2 (3) & 4 &	1	2 (3) & 4 &	1	2 (3)& (4)	(1) &(2)(3) & 4 &

Assignment 65 Play this chord riff on guitar or piano or with melodic instruments each playing a single note from each chord.

The whole effect was topped off by wailing gospel-style vocals and a blistering guitar solo.

Heavy rock seemed to have two main lyrical themes. First there was the blues-based lyric with its obvious sexuality. 'Love Hunter' by Whitesnake is an example of this:

> I need a woman to treat me good
> An' give me everything that a good woman should.
> Every day and every night
> She'd be waitin' on her brown-eyed boy
>   to come and treat her right.
> I'm a love hunter baby, sneaking up on you.

Assignment 66 Compose your own riff-based heavy rock number. Use bluesy lyrics, the blues scale (see page 13), and keep it simple.

The second lyrical theme was the fantasy-tale, a development from psychedelic rock, which involved mystical themes or mythical characters which would fit into a book like *Lord of the Rings*.

Assignment 67   Listen to 'Stairway to Heaven' by Led Zeppelin (on the *4 Symbols* album, Atlantic K 50008). Make a chart showing the instruments used in each verse.

Led Zeppelin, Black Sabbath and Deep Purple were the first heavy rock bands but they were followed by a multitude of others and the style has continued with little development, except perhaps for an increase in tempo, to the present day. Heavy rock has legions of followers and will probably last for a long time.

GLITTER ROCK

The other development of the early 1970s, **glitter rock**, faded out around 1975. The name grew out of the sequinned costumes of many of its stars and from the name of one of its leading lights, Gary Glitter.

Glitter rock had little that was new to offer music. It was a mishmash of styles developed in the 1960s with no really original or distinctive blend. Bands like T. Rex, Sweet, Gary Glitter and others, played boogie-blues in pop style, or light riff-music.

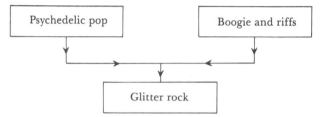

Led Zeppelin in full flight.

David Bowie.

DAVID BOWIE

David Bowie is one figure to come out of glitter rock who has developed and changed with popular music, often ahead of his time, and who has been a source of inspiration to others.

Bowie really did bring some fresh musical interest to the early seventies. He used a Cockney accent, taken from the singing of West End musical star Anthony Newley, at a time when many singers still used American accents. His songs often sounded as though they would fit into a stage musical; they had a real sense of drama and characterisation, and a decadent yet heroic flavour. His album *Ziggy Stardust*, named after a character invented by Bowie and acted by him during concerts, is the best example of this dramatic style. As an artist, Bowie has refused to stand still. Since *Ziggy Stardust* he has made albums incorporating disco (see page 82), funk (see page 85), experimental electronics and pop.

PUNK

With rock music becoming more and more artificial, with concert tickets becoming more and more expensive, with superstars singing songs which had little to do with teenage life on the streets and with economic depression setting in, it should have been obvious that a change was going to come. But when it did come in 1976, it caught everybody by surprise. The **punk** explosion, like the coming of rock'n'roll and the arrival of the Beatles, changed pop music.

Punk put into words the feelings of ordinary young people. The lyrics expressed disgust with the society they were part of. Taking an anarchist line, punk said that governments were corrupt and that people should govern themselves; that plastic TV culture was boring and that the kids were bored;

that society needed destroying; that working-class housing conditions were disgusting; that unemployment meant no future for working-class youth; that authority was fascist; that war was criminally stupid. Punk said these things crudely and simply. It was a successor to the protest-song idea dating back to Guthrie and before, but expressed with new venom and directness:

> God save the Queen
> The fascist regime
> There ain't no future
> In England's dream
> No future, no future, no future . . .

(From 'God save the Queen' by the Sex Pistols)

Johnny Rotten of the Sex Pistols.

The outrageous punk image was originally shrewdly manufactured by Malcolm McLaren, a clothes-shop owner and manager of the Sex Pistols. Everything about the Pistols was designed to shock, and not to be 'boring like the hippies'. McLaren took elements of all the most outrageous youth fashion-cults since the war and created a monster. Johnny Rotten, the Sex Pistols lead singer, would wear a teddy boy's drape jacket from the rock'n'roll era, a pin-collar shirt from the mod days, huge pin-striped trousers or tartans from Glitter rock vintage, all held together with safety-pins. The haircut was spiky and the face expressed a scowl or leer. Adults and the media were enraged again. Sex Pistols records were banned, their concerts were cancelled, they were attacked in the streets – and they had hit after hit.

The punk drug, like that of the mods (see page 56), was amphetamine, and punk music showed the same chaotic, high energy. It was very fast for the time (and has got faster as it has developed). The playing itself, the classic-rock line-up of guitars, bass and drums, is usually very basic. Bass-chords in the Chuck Berry vein are a common feature, the guitarist playing only down-strokes with the plectrum, often only on the bottom two strings.

Assignment 68

(a) Learn to play this guitar-line from 'God Save the Queen' by the Sex Pistols:

```
E E E E E E E    A A A A A A A A
A A A A A A A A  D D D C# C# C# D D
>     >     >    >     >     >
```

(b) Beat two drums, or other objects – the first pitched lower than the second – in time with the above guitar-line, like this:

```
        High        2  &      4  &  |        2  &      4  &  |
Count [ Low    1  &      3  &        | 1  &      3  &        |
               >     >     >     >     >     >     >     >
```

On the record the guitar part is relentless but syncopates the accents, in this case in a vicious, amplified parody of the rumba (see page 25). Behind this the drums play a brutally straight version of the 4/4 beat.

The punk guitar sound is usually heavily distorted to give a 'buzz-saw' effect. There are seldom any guitar solos, and what solo lines there are, are usually very simple, consisting of a two-to-four-note riff, or a distorted parody of a Chuck Berry solo.

The melody-line of the songs is commonly a mixture of shouted chants on two to four notes (e.g. 'God Save the Queen'). The singing is usually in a British accent (more raucous than Bowie's), and uses the major scale. Afro-Americanisms like blue-notes are played less often by punk bands.

The structure of the songs is very simple. While many punk bands soon moved beyond these narrow boundaries, the basics themselves proved very effective.

Assignment 69   Listen to side one of the Sex Pistols' first LP *Never Mind the Bollocks* (Virgin records V2086). List which of the basic ingredients are used in which songs, and which songs go beyond these and how.

Assignment 70   Write your own punk song. Include these ingredients:
1   Simple major chords played bass-chord fashion as above.
2   A chanted melody-line based on up to four notes from a major scale.
3   Angry protest-style lyrics.

One thing punk achieved was the establishment of a number of small record labels and alternative record distribution chains like Rough Trade. At first,

Siouxsie and the Banshees.

the record industry felt threatened but punk's major acts, the Sex Pistols, the Clash, the Buzzcocks, X-Ray Specs, Generation X and Siouxsie and the Banshees, all signed to major companies. The Sex Pistols managed to get sacked by two record companies, A&M and EMI, before finally settling with Virgin.

The Sex Pistols soon burnt out. Johnny Rotten left the group after the first US tour. Paul Cook and Steve Jones remained with Sid Vicious as the front man. Vicious died from a heroin overdose while awaiting trial for the murder of his girlfriend, Nancy Spungen. The Clash took over the lead of the movement, but after a string of excellent punk albums – *The Clash*, *Give 'Em Enough Rope*, and *London Calling* – they moved towards reggae and funk.

A few bands continued the punk tradition. Much of it was such fast and shouted noise that it has been dubbed 'Oi music'. Some of its exponents are the Angelic Upstarts and Sham 69.

NEW WAVE (1977)

New wave music didn't have the same anarchist intention and social concerns as punk. New wave records sounded more polished, were better produced and showed a higher standard of musicianship. As with punk, the songs were short and full of energy, but they were definitely pop music again.

The songs of the new wave were about the main pop concerns – boys and girls and their relationships. Listen to the lyrics of groups like Graham Parker and the Rumour, Blondie, the Pretenders, the Boomtown Rats. There were exceptions, like Elvis Costello, who tried to carry on the Dylan lyrics tradition, but they were few and far between. However, new wave is often very good pop, well written, intelligent, with a hard, clean, rock-group sound; there are no slushy strings, though there is the occasional synthesiser or keyboard.

New wave is too diverse to classify more tightly than this in musical terms. It ranges from street-punk style ('Denis, Denis' by Blondie) to white reggae ('Roxanne', by the Police; 'Watching the Detectives', by Elvis Costello). Each band seems to have drawn from a mixture of slightly different musical roots.

REVIVALS

Following the demise of punk in 1979, the charts went through two or three years of revivals of earlier styles in Britain. There were mod revivals (The Jam, Secret Affair), heavy rock revivals (Motorhead, Judas Priest, Saxon), and rockabilly revivals (Shakin' Stevens, Stray Cats). Few lasted long or made much impact. A new black and white mix was needed.

Music to hear

Heavy rock: *Led Zeppelin*, Atlantic 588171.
Led Zeppelin 4, Atlantic 2401012 K50008.
Paranoid, Black Sabbath, Vertigo 6360 011.
Fireball, Deep Purple, Harvest SHVL 793.

Glitter rock: *Greatest Hits*, Vol. 1, T. Rex, Pickwick PDA044.
Elton's Greatest Hits, Elton John, DJM DJLPH 442.
Rise and Fall of Ziggy Stardust, David Bowie, RCA 443 051.
Diamond Dogs, David Bowie, RCA APLI 0576.

Punk rock: *The Clash*, CBS 82000.
Never Mind the Bollocks, The Sex Pistols, Virgin V2086.
Give 'Em Enough Rope, The Clash, CBS 82341.

Oi music: *That's Life*, Sham 69, Polydor POLD 5010 2442 158.

New wave: *Best of Blondie*, Chrysalis CDL TV1.
This Year's Model, Elvis Costello, Radar RAD 3.
Regatta de Blanc, Police, A&M AMLH64792.

10 Hit Me With Music: From reggae to funk

Rastafarian drummers. Rastafarianism, a complex religion developed among blacks in the Caribbean, draws on the historical roots of black people in Africa. Drumming is considered to be a religious activity.

Black music in the 1970s had several main strands. The Tamla Motown sound (see page 48) moved on to become disco, the soul sound (see page 49) became funk, and new sounds arrived from Jamaica in the form of reggae and ska.

Slavery had flourished in the Caribbean just as it had in North and South America. Here, the music that developed from the black/white, African/European mix, took the form of work songs and spirituals (see chapter 1), and led to styles of music unique to the Caribbean such as **mento** and **calypso**.

MENTO

Mento is the national dance of Jamaica and uses a rhythm which it shares with the calypso (see below) and rumba (see page 25). This is the lively, syncopated rhythm which results when quavers are grouped like this: 3 + 3 + 2. (You can see the rhythm written out on the opposite page.) Mento songs are sung in the Jamaican dialect-language, and their words deal with local issues and themes of protest and satire. (The dialect-languages used in the various Caribbean islands are each different one from another although they are all based on one, or a mixture of more than one, of the languages imported by the European settlers. These dialect-languages were originally used by the slaves as a means of communicating with each other without the settlers being able to understand.)

CALYPSO

Calypso songs come from Trinidad and Tobago and use the dialect-language of that part of the Caribbean. They are faster and lighter-sounding than mento songs but deal with the same kinds of themes. Calypso songs in the dialect-languages of other eastern Caribbean islands are now also common.

Assignment 71   Clap, or tap out the $3+3+2$ rhythm of mento and calypso, putting the stress on the quaver counts of 1, 4 and 7:

$$\frac{4}{4} \quad \downarrow. \qquad \downarrow. \qquad \downarrow$$

Count 1 (2) (3)   4   (5) (6)   7 (8)

SKA   Jamaican popular music began in Kingston during the 1950s with the arrival of people from the countryside seeking work in the city. These new arrivals lived in wooden shanty towns but many had transistor radios and could tune in to pop radio stations in the USA. The music they heard included blues, jazz, gospel and particularly the R'n'B of the North American black people. Jamaican disc jockeys got hold of these American records and played them on their travelling discos or 'sound-systems'. Jamaican musicians began playing their own style of R'n'B, mixing ideas from the original Afro-American music with rhythms from their own Jamaican folk music. It was from this mixture that **ska** was eventually formed. Its early stars were Jimmy Cliff and Desmond Dekker.

Ska came to Britain with West Indian immigrants and was taken up by the skinheads, usually poor working-class whites, who identified with it. In the mid-1960s there were some ska hits in Britain like 'My Boy Lollipop' by Millie and Dekker's 'Israelites'.

Jamaican ska singer Jimmy Cliff.

Ska has a fast dance-rhythm. Each off-beat quaver is picked out by the guitar and hi-hat:

Count (1) & (2) & (3) & (4) &

while the bass-guitar and drums play a rhythm which accents the off-beat, for example:

Rhythm

Beat

Assignment 72

Form three groups and use different percussion instruments to play the ska rhythm-parts shown above (including the guitar/hi-hat rhythm and the beat).

Assignment 73

Work out the tune of 'Ob-la-di, Ob-la-da' by the Beatles (on *The Beatles 1967–70*, Parlophone PCSP 718), and accompany it in ska style.

ROCK STEADY

Around 1966, the very similar, but slower **rock steady** took over from ska in Jamaica. Whereas the lyrics of ska are mainly about love and making love, rock steady is about the police, hungry children and politics.

TWO TONE

In 1979 ska enjoyed a brief revival in the hands of the groups on a small independent record label called **Two tone**, based in Coventry, England. The lyrics of two-tone songs were closer to punk but, rhythmically, some of the groups were developing the ska beat. Two-tone groups included the Specials, the Selecter, the Body-snatchers, Madness, Bad Manners, and the Beat.

Assignment 74

Here is an example of the rhythmic complexity of two tone based on 'Hands Off She's Mine' by the Beat. Use whatever instruments you have, trying to get as close to the sounds of the original instruments as possible, and learn to play it:

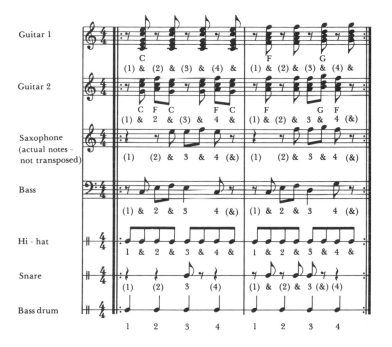

'Uprising', *Bob Marley and the Wailers, record sleeve.*

REGGAE

Rock steady was a transitional music and by 1968 it was replaced by **reggae**. Reggae is the music of the 'rude boys', the outlaws of Kingston, Jamaica's capital. Rude boys are street punks and were often members of criminal gangs. Reggae is also the music of another set of outlaws in Jamaica, the Rastafarians. Rastas believe that one day black people will return to their promised land, the country of Ethiopia in Africa. They also believe in peace, love and brotherhood. They smoke marijuana (cannabis) as a 'holy herb'. Reggae songs began by reflecting these things, plus the struggle against the injustice of the corrupt western civilisation (called Babylon by the Rastas), which white industrial society, with its rat-race and corruption, represents.

The slow rhythm of reggae is difficult to represent in musical form because its basic unit of rhythm is somewhere between this: ♩. ♪ which goes with a $\frac{4}{4}$ time signature, and ♪♪ which goes with a $\frac{12}{8}$ time signature. This book will use the $\frac{4}{4}$ version.

Here is an example of a reggae rhythm. The important thing to note is that the first beat in the bar is a rest for most of the instruments playing the accompaniment:

Assignment 75

Practise the above rhythms on whatever instruments you have, with the melodic instruments each playing a single note from the chord of C.

Assignment 76

Using chords I, IV, V, VI, compose a reggae song and accompaniment. Write the lyrics either about peace and love or about some social problem. You can use either a major scale or a blues scale.

Bob Marley was reggae's first international star. His songs were truly Rastafarian and strongly political. Because of Marley and artists like U-Roy, Bunny Wailer, Toots and the Maytals, Burning Spear and Eddie Grant, elements of reggae have started to appear in mainstream chart music. The rhythm has been used and coupled to rock arrangements by the Police and other British bands. Reggae 'dub' recording techniques involve creative blending of the instrument volume-levels in the recording 'mix' and the use of echo effects on various instruments and drums. 'Dub' is now used in the recording of disco, funk and other popular styles.

Bob Marley with Rastafarian dreadlocks. Marley brought the reel music of Kingston, Jamaica to world attention.

PHILLIE SOUL

Black music in the USA during the 1970s built on the Tamla Motown and soul sounds of the sixties. Motown faded from the limelight and its brand of black pop/soul found a new base in Philadelphia in the early 1970s. **Phillie soul**, as it was known, was a much smoother cocktail bar music. It was very successful throughout the seventies. Bands like the O Jays, the Three Degrees, and the Delfonics had a string of hits. The Stylistics had hits which included 'You Make Me Feel Brand New', and 'I'm Stone in Love with You'. The harmonies were silkier than in Motown recordings; the feel was much more relaxed.

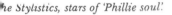

he Stylistics, stars of 'Phillie soul'.

During the 1960s black music was valued for its feeling, for the emotional force of the singing. By the late sixties and early seventies white artists like Janis Joplin, right down to popular TV stars like Tom Jones, were singing in soulful style, but often without any real commitment to the lyrics. Heavy-rock singers had also borrowed the gospel type of vocals. Black singers and musicians had dropped the wilder side of soul singing for a cooler sound that was less expressive.

DISCO

Disco is, in a sense, the culmination of this move away from gospel emotion. It started out, around 1974, as the music that was played in private clubs and discothèques in New York and other places. What was important was neither the melody nor the instrumentation but the dance value of the rhythm. The songs were sometimes reduced to a superficial type of treatment. Disco was described in one US music paper as 'a mix of jogging, the swinging bar, the drug high, and light show . . .'.

Disco-rhythms

You can do almost any modern dance to the basic rhythm. The disco beat is a straight $\frac{4}{4}$, unsyncopated and with its basic rhythm picked out by the rhythm guitar and hi-hat:

Count 1 & a 2 & a 3 & a 4 & a

*The Hippodrome, London –
'hyper-disco'.*

82

Assignment 77

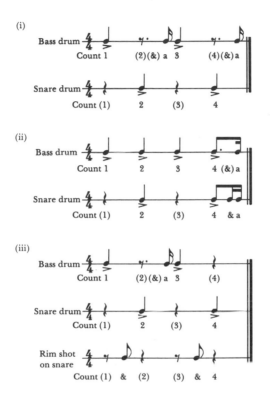

(a) Tap out the basic disco-rhythm shown above.

(b) Here are some variations on the disco-rhythm. Divide into small groups and learn to play them. Add the basic disco-rhythm over the top with guitar or hi-hat. Notice that while all four beats are accented, the bass drum accentuates beats 1 and 3, and the snare emphasises beats 2 and 4.

Disco styles

Donna Summer was the first artist to be recognised as a disco star. Her 1976 single 'Love to Love You Baby' gained notoriety because of the singer's moaning over the backing track. The Tamla Motown soul and Phillie soul sounds had been combined with a disco beat. Donna Summer was followed in the soul-disco market by other black artists like the Ohio Players, Gloria Gaynor, Barry White, the Ritchie Family and Shalamar.

It was not long before disco really caught on in Europe and European artists – both black and white, but mainly white – began to make disco records. Eurodisco was bland and sterile in the main. Based on the fact that anything fits a disco beat, the Europeans put a particularly manufactured brand of pop music to it. Artists in the Eurodisco field include Sheila B. Devotion, Chic, Amanda Lear, Luv, and Silver Connection, as well as much of ABBA's output.

Disco queen Donna Summer.

Shortly after this, the film *Saturday Night Fever*, with the **Bee Gees'** brand of disco, came out and soon everyone was making disco records. Stars like Rod Stewart and the Rolling Stones produced rock-disco tracks. Eurodisco ran to tracks lasting the whole side of an album with different moods, played by an orchestra. Another trend was to put oldies to a disco beat; showbiz songs, rock, soul, gospel, and the works of classical composers were arranged and 'put to disco'.

Disco was a style that many people dabbled in, while producing most of their work in the allied fields of soul, pop, reggae, and most often, funk. The link with funk also led to the 'rapping' on many disco records, where the singer (originally the DJ) speaks rhythmic rhymes (originally improvised) against an instrumental backing.

Assignment 78

Record a disco beat and invent your own 'rap' about school or your friends. Make your lines rhyme in pairs and make them either one or two bars long. Deliver them with rhythmic punch, emphasising syllables which land directly on the beat (i.e. on a count of 1, 2, 3, 4).

John Travolta, star of the film
Saturday Night Fever.

FUNK

If Motown and Phillie soul originally inspired disco, so Atlantic and Stax soul inspired **funk**. Certainly James Brown moved from soul to become one of funk's originators. However, funk, which has many styles, also has jazz, rock and blues influences, often difficult to unravel and often varying from one area of the USA to another.

In the jazz dictionary, funky means 'dirty' music having a blues feeling and distorted tone on the instruments. Ask a funk musician to 'play funky' and he will start to play blue notes and syncopated rhythms. These form the basis of funk style and were first found in the music of James Brown.

James Brown and the J.B.s' style started in the mid-1960s and developed into the early 1970s. It consists of rhythmic bright-sounding guitars; quick runs from brass instruments; broken percussive bass-lines; clipped, rhythmic accents on the drums. Over this goes the rhythmic, punctuated vocal-line in wild, gospel-based style. These make up the bedrock of funk. Funk is black dance-music, raw and undiluted.

Jimi Hendrix, the 'psychedelic rock' guitarist, together with drummer Buddy Miles, increasingly turned to funk experimentation as his career went on, and this mixture of psychedelic music with funk has also been developed in the seventies.

James Brown.

The first funk band to reach mass audiences was Kool and the Gang, who had dance hits with carefree songs like 'Jungle Boogie', 'Funky Stuff' and 'Hollywood Swinging' in 1974. George Clinton has followed up both the straighter and more rock-orientated styles of funk with his bands Parliament and Funkadelic. Clinton borrowed the space-age clothing from glitter rock (see page 69), and his bands' songs reflected the decadence of American inner-cities. The guitar-lines were extensions of Hendrix's jazzy and rhythmic experiments.

Earth, Wind And Fire avoided the psychedelic influence and instead incorporated elements of mainstream jazz, Motown and Phillie soul, and African rhythms. The rhythmic complexity of the band – a move closer to its African roots – in the drums, bass and guitar departments, is covered with lush strings and harmony vocals.

Features of funk

There are several features common to all styles of funk. The bass-lines of funk have now moved well into the mainstream of popular music. The distinctive popping bass-guitar sound, caused by slapping the strings, on many records has been derived from funk. Like other musical ingredients of funk, the bass-line must be rhythmic, syncopated, percussive.

The rhythm guitar in funk plays a similar role. It plays short rhythmic riffs based on the blues scale. These are not played in step with the bass guitar, but cut across it, giving a strong polyrhythmic feel (see page 2). The chords used in funk are often similar to those used in jazz.

Assignment 79   Play this funk chord-sequence on guitar, keyboard, or a combination of
melody instruments, or just tap out the rhythm.

Count 1   2   (3)   4   1   2   (3)   4

Play very slowly at first and gradually work up speed.

The brass section (or 'horns') play riffs and full chords as they did in soul, but
in funk the riffs are quicker and often quite short.

Assignment 80   Play this funky horn riff on whatever instrument you feel most comfortable
with.

Count 1   2   3   (4)   (1)   2   3   (4)

*Talking Heads, one of the most
intelligent and subversive
modern groups.*

In the 1980s white bands began to play funk. One of the first of these was Talking Heads. Their mastermind, David Byrne, has collaborated with Brian Eno, the synthesiser wizard from the early Roxy Music. Their albums with Eno combined African rhythms and synthesised sounds with funky bass-lines and vocal-lines.

Assignment 81

The following rhythm part shows how complex modern funk rhythms have become. Play it in the following ways.

(a)　With a different untuned percussion instrument for each part.

(b)　With tuned instruments playing a common single note for parts 1, 2, 3, 4 and 5.

(c)　With a bass guitar playing a three-note, blues-scale riff using the rhythm of part 1. With a guitar playing another three-note, blues-scale riff using the rhythm of part 2. With a guitar playing a simple chord riff using part 3. With keyboards and/or brass and wind instruments playing chords or three-note, blues-scale riffs based on parts 4 and 5.

These parts must be carefully composed so that when they are built up part by part during playing, they fit together musically.

Music to hear   Ska and rock steady: *Best of Jimmy Cliff*, Island ICD 6.
                                          Israelites, Desmond Dekker, Cactus.
                                          Ska Authentic, the Skalites, Studio One.
                    Two tone: *The Specials*, Two tone CDL TT 5001.
                                I Just Can't Stop It, the Beat Go Feet, BEAT 001.
                    Reggae: *African Herbsman*, Bob Marley, Trojan TRL62.
                              Legalize It, Peter Tosh, Columbia PC 34253.
                              Black Heart Man, Bunny Wailer, Island ILPS 941.
                              Marcus Garvey, Burning Spear, Island ILPS 9377.
                              Exodus, Bob Marley, Island ILPS 9498.
                    Phillie Soul: *Greatest Hits*, O Jays, Philadelphia 86058.
                                    'I'm Stone In Love With You', the Stylistics, Avco
                                    6105 015.
                                    'You Make Me Feel Brand New', the Stylistics, Avco
                                    6105 028.
                    Disco: (Soul) 'Love to Love You Baby', Donna Summer, GTO
                             GT 17.
                             'The Best Disco in Town', Ritchie Family, Polydor
                             2058 777.
                             (Funk) 'Le Freak', Chic, Atlantic K11209.
                             (Rock) 'Do Ya Think I'm Sexy', Rod Stewart, Warner
                             Bros, 8724.
                             (Euro) 'Knowing Me, Knowing You', ABBA, Epic
                             EPC 4955.
                             (Pop) 'Saturday Night Fever', Bee Gees, RSO 4955.
                    Funk: *Funkenstein vs the Placebo Syndrome*, Parliament,
                            Casablanca CALN 2021.
                            One Nation Under a Groove, Funkadelic, WB K
                            56539.
                            That's the Way of The World, Earth, Wind And Fire,
                            Columbia 33280.

THE FUTURE

The music of the new romantics and futurists which appeared in the early 1980s blended new ideas with elements of earlier styles. The vocal style of hip-hop (break-dancing) was a development of the 'rapping' of some reggae and funk.

Assignment 82

Listen to songs from a selection of bands currently in the charts.
(a)   As you listen to each group make a list of musical influences you hear from earlier styles of music.
(b)   Compare the lists. Do they have elements in common? Can you distinguish which influences are from black, and which from white music?

The 1980s have seen the ever increasing power of record producers like Trevor Horn, who play a major role in every stage of the creation of a record. Only one thing is certain about the future: music will develop new forms, blending elements of black and white music in dynamic fashion, and these new forms will in turn be shaped by technology, social change and commercial demands. Such is the nature of popular music.

Some suggestions for further reading

Michael Burnett	*Pop Music*	Oxford University Press.
	Jamaican Music	Oxford University Press.
	Jazz	Oxford University Press.
Graham Collier	*Jazz*	Cambridge University Pre
Avril Dankworth	*Jazz: An Introduction to Its Musical Basis*	Oxford University Press.
Stephen Davies & Peter Simon	*Reggae Bloodlines*	Heinemann Educational.
Simon Frity	*Soul and Motown*	Routledge & Kegan Paul.
Peter Gammond	*Scott Joplin and the Ragtime Era*	Abacus.
Hilary Hayward	*Careers in the Music Business*	Kogan Page.
George Martin	*Making Music*	Muller.
Paul Oliver	*The Story of the Blues*	Penguin.
Jeremy Pascall	*The Illustrated History of Pop Music*	Hamlyn.
Dave Rogers	*Rock'n'Roll*	Routledge & Kegan Paul.
John Shepherd	*Tin Pan Alley*	Routledge & Kegan Paul.
John Tobler	*Punk Rock*	Phoebus.

Acknowledgements

BBC Hulton Picture Library, pages 1, 8, 11 (left), 15, 16, 22, 26, 31, 34; British Library, page 11 (right); Country Music, page 33; Hippodrome, London, page 82; London Features International, pages 40 (left), 41, 47 (left & right), 50, 60, 67, 69, 70, 81 (bottom), 84; Melody Maker, pages 12, 26, 40 (right), 43; National Film Archive, pages 35, 85; The Photo Source, pages 56, 58; Rastafarian Information Service, page 76; David Redfern, page 53; Rex Features, pages 49 (left & right), 54, 61, 71, 73, 77, 81 (top), 86, 87; Topham, page 3; Wide World, pages 39, 63; Val Wilmer, pages 2, 18, 28, 29.